Blue Macaw

Blue Macaws as Pets

Blue Macaw book for Keeping, Pros and Cons, Care, Housing, Diet and Health.

By

Donald Sunderland

Table of Contents

Introduction

Macaws are among the most beautiful birds in the world. They are known for their majestic plumes and their extremely high intelligence that makes them the perfect pet. Among these birds are the blue macaws. Most often people refer to the Hyacinth macaw when talking about blue macaws. However, there are four known species of blue macaws. Sadly, only two of these species have come to become popular pets while the other two have been under threat because of poaching. These species do not do very well in captivity either, leading to extremely low numbers.

This book will help you learn in detail about all the species of blue macaws. It is a guide for new bird owners and those with some experience to provide the right care for their pet birds.

While blue macaws are very intelligent, these birds can be quite a handful if you do not know how to keep them healthy and stimulated. The diet, ample exercise and proper living conditions are essential to keeping your macaw happy and healthy.

There are also several safety guidelines that you need to follow when you bring your pet bird home. The most common household items can pose a big threat to your bird. Making sure that your house is bird proofed correctly is also extremely essential.

With this book, you will get an insight into all the aspects of taking care of your blue macaw. From choosing your bird to making correct and safe introductions, the book covers everything. All the tips are presented in a manner that is easy for you to understand. They are also extremely practical as they are based on the experience of previous macaw owners.

The information provided is based on extensive research to provide you with information that is authentic. Being a bird owner is a great responsibility. These birds live for a good 15-50 years, depending upon the species. So, you need to be entirely ready in order to make a commitment.

This book also tells you how to know if you are ready to be a macaw owner. It highlights the difficulties that macaw owners face with their pets. It also highlights the responsibilities of a macaw owner.

That way, you can make an informed decision about whether you are really ready for a macaw or not. In case you feel uncertain, you always have the option of fostering a bird and taking good care of him. Once you know that you have the experience, you can bring one into your home.

There is no doubt that Blue Macaws are magnificent creatures. Once you have them figured out, they can be wonderful companions. They are also extremely entertaining as they are curious and playful beings. It is necessary for you to provide the right care to bring out the best in your bird.

Chapter 1: Blue Macaws as Pets

Macaws come in a variety of beautiful colors. Among the several species are the Blue Macaws. While the most popular of them all is the Hyacinth Macaw, there are three more species of blue macaws. Sadly two of them, the Spix Macaw and the Glaucous Macaw, are close to becoming extinct because of extensive poaching and their inability to breed well in captivity.

In fact, a Spix macaw named Presley, who inspired the animated film "Rio" died recently. He is believed to be the last of all the wild-born Spix Macaws.

Here is an overview of the spectacular Blue Macaw species

1. The four blues
The four species of blue macaws that are known include:

a. Spix Macaw

Overview: Today there are less than 100 Spix Macaws remaining in the wild. These birds are believed to be extinct in the wild due to loss of habitat and wildlife trafficking. For this reason, these birds have been listed as Critically Endangered by the IUCN. They are popularly known as the 'little blue macaw'.

These birds live for about 28-29 years on average.

Range and habitat: These birds are native to Brazil in South America. They mostly inhabited the north-eastern part of Bahia and southern Piaui. It is also likely that populations existed in the western part of Pernambuca, Southern Maranhai and the north eastern part of Goias.

These birds are normally found in Caraibeira ripiran woodlands. They are also found in a semi-arid habitat called the Caatinga. These birds usually inhabit the Carribean Trumpet Trees and the buriti palm trees.

Physical characteristics:

- They are the smallest of all the blue macaws.

- These birds are identified by the eye rings and the featherless grey skin on the facial region.
- The bird grows to a length of about 56 cms.
- Male and female birds are identical in appearance. However, the male birds are heavier and larger than the females.
- The head has a distinct blue-grey plumage.
- The underparts are pale blue with some feathers that are vivid blue.
- The tail and wings are vivid blue in color.
- The feet and legs are brownish-black in color while the beak is dark grey in color.
- As for juveniles, they are quite similar to the adults but have facial skin that is pale grey. The iris is brown and there is a distinct white stripe that stretches from the top of the beak, along the centre.

b. Glaucous Macaw

Overview: The Glaucous Macaw does not have any reliable sighting records since 1960. However, certain rumors of the bird being spotted recently have prevented the bird from being listed extinct officially.

The last known bird in captivity was seen alive in 1936 when it was on exhibit in the Buenos Aires Gardens. Another such specimen was seen in the Jardin d' Acclimation in Paris between 1895 and 1905.

Deforestation is the main cause of the extinction of these birds. Palm groves that are the main habitat have been cleared exhaustively for agriculture.

In addition to this, there are speculations of a disease outbreak and also poaching for feathers and trafficking.

Range and Habitat:

The glaucous macaw has a very localized range. They are found in the south eastern part of South America. These birds were widely found along the middle reaches of prominent rivers.

The range extends from the border of Brazil to north eastern Argentina and the south eastern part of Paraguay. They have also been sighted in the northern parts of Uruguay. Some rare sightings have also been recorded in the lower parts of Paraguay and the Parana River.

These birds have commonly been spotted near rivers. This is probably because during the time that these records were made, boats were the primary mode of transport. Very little access was available to the interiors of the region inhabited by these birds. So, there are also some assumptions that these birds lived in the sub-tropical forests that bordered these rivers.

The main source of food for these birds are palm nuts. Therefore it is quite likely that a few flocks lived near forests where these trees were commonly found. This includes lightly wooded areas and also the palm savannahs in South America.

Physical characteristics:

- This is a large sized bird, growing up to 70 cms in length.
- The name Glaucous comes from the Latin word Glaucus which means green or bluish green. This refers to the pale grey and bluish appearance of the plumes of this bird.
- The head is large and greyish in color.
- The rest of the body is covered in turquoise blue plumes.
- The eye-ring is yellow and bare.
- The lappets that are moon shaped are found along the mandibles. This is a unique physical trait of this bird.
- The beak is large and extremely strong and is black or dark grey in color.

c. Lear's Macaw

Overview: The Lear's Macaw is also called the indigo macaw. It is a large bird that was described for the first time in the year 1856. These birds have been named after Edward Lear who recorded the birds extensively with paintings and drawings of birds in the zoos.

When the bird was exhibited in 1950 in the Brazilian Zoo for the first time, it was believed to be a hybrid because of its similarity to the hyacinth macaw. It was only in 1978 that this bird was recognized as a separate species when ornithologist Helmut Sick discovered wild populations when he was in Bahia in the north eastern part of Brazil.

Range and distribution

These birds are native to Brazil. However, the range is quite small including only Bahia and parts of the Pernambuco states. There are two populations of these birds that are currently known. One of them is in the Toca Velha in Canudos and the other one is in Serra Branca in Jeremaobo.

There was a population of 22 birds that was found between Campo Formoso and Sento Se. However, it is believed that these were only migratory birds that came from the locations mentioned above. These birds visited the area for the fruits of the Syagrus plant.

These birds are commonly found in the arid and open areas of the caatinga habitat. These areas are filled with thorn bushes and cliffs made of sandstone. Both are ideal for the roosting and nesting conditions needed by these birds.

Physical characteristics:

- These birds grow to a length of about 70-81 cms.
- They weigh close to 1 kilo, with an average of 950 g.
- They have an orange yellow eye ring.
- One distinct characteristic is a patch of bare skin near the lower mandible that is pale yellow in color.
- They have a heavy beak that is black in color.
- The legs and feet are dark grey in color.
- The iris is dark brown in color.
- They have a brilliant cobalt blue plumage. In the sun, this plumage looks extremely glossy and vibrant.
- The feathers on the chest, head, belly and neck are greenish blue in color.
- The feathers on the back and the wings are black in color.
- Males and females look almost identical, except for the larger beak in the females.
- As for the juveniles the beak is paler and the tail is a lot shorter. They also have a lighter yellow patch of pale skin.

d. Hyacinth Macaw

Overview: The hyacinth macaws are the largest flighted birds. The populations of these birds in the wild are quite low and are only a few, countable thousands. Since these birds became extremely popular as pets, trafficking and pet trade have taken a toll on the wild populations. Many of these birds have even disappeared from their natural ranges entirely.

Not only are these birds beautiful, they are also extremely playful and goofy. As a result, more and more homes have brought them in as pets. Of course, captive breeding efforts have been made to keep the populations intact.

Distribution and range

These birds formerly inhabited the entire stretch from the northern part of Brazil to the northern parts of the Amazon. This included Rio Tapajos in the west, Southern Brazil, southern parts of Maranhao, Minas Gerias, Western parts of Bahia, north eastern Paraguay and east Bolivia.

Today, these birds have disappeared from most of these natural ranges. They are mostly found in three locations, namely South Brazil, North East Paraguay and East Bolivia.

These birds are mostly found in semi-open and open areas that contain tall trees. They prefer savannah areas with palm trees, cerrado vegetation and any flooded area that contain the buriti palm groves. Rather than the rain forests, these birds are found in gallery forests and in the edges of forests.

During the day, these birds fly long distances in search of their favorite foods. They roost in the tall palms and trees.

Physical description

- It is the largest flighted bird growing to a length of 40 inches.
- They weigh between 1.2- 1.5 kilograms.
- The body feathers are solid blue in color.
- The wings are a darker shade of blue.
- As for the undersides of the wings and the tail, the plumes are black in color.
- They have extremely strong beaks that can even bend wrought iron.

- The lower part of the mandible has bright yellow markings on the side.
- The circle around the eye is bright yellow too.
- They do not have any featherless patch of skin around the eye, like most macaws.
- The feet and legs are dark grey in color and the iris is dark brown in color.
- The male and female birds look identical. Of course, the female is more slender than the male.
- As for the juveniles the tail is shorter and the upper beak is paler.

2. History of Macaws as pets

The earliest known records of macaws were written by Lyndon L Hargrove. He talks about these birds in his book, Mexican Macaws Comparitive Osteology. This book was written in the year 1970.

His notes talk in detail of the Indians living in Arizona and New Mexico. As early as 1536, these people traded the feathers of macaws and other parrots in exchange for green stones.

Later on, a Spanish priest named Padre Verlarde wrote about the Pima Indians who domesticated these birds. His accounts that date back to 1716 state that these birds were primarily raised for their feathers. These colorful feathers were used as adornments. There are several documents available to support the fact that these birds were raised for their beautiful feathers. Another tribe named the Pueblo Indians also used the feathers of these birds as ornaments.

These birds were also highly revered and were often associated with high morals. It was a common belief that a person who had a poor character could never keep a scarlet or red macaw.

There are several interesting folklores of these birds. One such story is about the plucking of red feathers from the body of the bird. The region that the feather was plucked from was later inoculated with a fluid that was derived from a toad or frog. It is said that the feather that grew in its place had a tint of orange and bright yellow. These feathers carried great value even if the feather shaft was temporarily damaged.

In the Western world, Macaws grew in popularity as pets only around the early 20th century. They were imported in large numbers during this time. It was during the World Wars that these pet birds were very highly affected. The wars lead to the breakout of several bird diseases. When air transport became easier to access after the Second World War, these birds grew in popularity again. People were able to import these birds to keep as pets. Of course, macaws became popular because of their colorful and vibrant feathers.

Today, these birds cannot be imported as there are several laws restricting it. Since the numbers in the wild began to decline after their demand as pets increased, laws were put in place to protect numbers. Today, these birds are mostly bred in captivity and are then made available to those who want to keep them as pets.

Brief history of the four blues:

- **Spix Macaw:** These birds are named after Johann Baptist von Spix. In April 1819, he collected the first specimen of this bird in Juazerio along the Sao Francisco River. The bird was sighted next after a long gap of 84 years by Othmar reiser in the year 1903. These birds were only studied around the 1970s. They were later captured in 1987 for trade. A male and female spix macaw were discovered at this site around the 1990s. The female was released and sadly crashed into a power line. The male just vanished from the site. This was believed to mark the extinction of this species in the wild.

- **Glaucous Macaw:** The Glaucous Macaw is one of the most poorly reported ones of the four blues. The only reliable records were found dated around the 1960s. Even the residents of the area that the birds inhabited only had records that went back to the 1870s. Interest in the bird spiked after a possibility of extinction came into the forefront. This is when a few expeditions were carried out by ornithologists to Paraguay around the 1990s. These expeditions failed. This lead to beliefs that the bird is, in fact, extinct. However, George Smith presented several talks about macaws in which he stated that these birds were not extinct but were found in more remote areas of Bolivia.

- **Lear's macaw:** This species was described for the first time in the year 1856 by Charles Lucien Bonaparte, the French ornithologist. Since these birds were sighted very rarely, they were often confused with the Hyacinth macaw. That is why they were not considered a different species until 1978. This is when they were located in the wild by Helmut Sick. As mentioned before, these birds were named after Edward Lear. He captured several images and paintings of these birds in his book the *Illustrations of the Family of Psittacidae.* Till they were spotted in the wild, these paintings were believed to be those of Hyacinth Macaws.

- **Hyacinth Macaws:** These birds were first described in the year 1790 by John Latham, an English ornithologist, physician and artist. They were kept as pets around the early 1900s. These birds became popular instantly. They were able to entertain and were also very affectionate towards their families. Today, these birds are bred in captivity all over the globe.

3. Macaws: Good, bad and ugly

Macaws make great pets without a doubt. However, these birds tend to be noisy and may be difficult for first time bird owners. The sheer size of the birds can make behavior issues like nipping quite dangerous.

If you are planning to bring home a macaw, there are several considerations that you need to make before committing to the bird. This includes the expenses involved, the care, the possible behavioral issues and even health issues.

Here is a detailed list of the good, the bad and the ugly that comes with being a macaw owner so that you can make an informed decision.

Things to consider

Before you commit to a macaw, you must understand that it takes more than just leaving food in a cage. These birds are demanding in certain ways and you must be entirely ready to provide them with a home that lets them thrive.

If you are seriously contemplating brining a macaw home, here are a few things that you must consider:

- **They can be very noisy:** Macaws are noisy at intervals. This means that they will be quiet for a long time and will let out ear piercing squeaks from time to time. Macaws are considered to be the most vocal of all the parrot species. This is because, in the wild, these birds travel far and wide in search of food. They use their loud vocalization to communicate with their flock mates. This is an instinct that you can expect in your pet bird too.
- **They are messy:** While a clean environment is necessary for the macaws to stay healthy, they can be messy as a species. They will leave food bits lying around everywhere. They even fling their food from time to time, ruining your walls. Of course, you cannot ignore the debris left behind by their toys.

- **You have to make changes in your schedule:** You need to be dedicated to your macaws. This starts with training, feeding and even cleaning the bird and its environment. Macaws are very intelligent birds, which also means that they need a lot of mental stimulation. This is achieved through play, which requires your time. You will have to prepare meals, follow a good feeding schedule and even set time aside to play with your bird to keep him happy.

- **Variety in diet:** Only seeds and pellets are not good enough for your macaw. You will also need to spend some time preparing fresh food with fruits and vegetables. When the bird has a good source of nutrition, you can avoid behavioral issues, mood swings, health issues and other common problems.

- **You must invest in toys:** Macaws need a variety of toys. This keeps them mentally stimulated. Birds that are bored will resort to screaming, biting or feather plucking.

- **There are expenses involved:** To begin with, blue macaws are expensive birds. Besides this, you have to invest in a good cage, toys, veterinary care and a lot more. In the following chapters we will discuss the several costs involved so that you can be sure that you can make the commitment.

- **They can be hazardous:** Macaws are large birds. This makes them a risky pet to have. They rely extensively on instinct since they are prey animals. While they are easier to handle as babies, an adult macaw can cause a lot of damage with his powerful beak and toes.

- **You cannot smoke:** For smokers, bringing a bird home means that they need to be additionally cautious. The respiratory system of your bird is extremely sensitive. They will develop issues like feather plucking when constantly exposed to smoke.

- **It is a commitment of a lifetime:** Blue macaws live for an average of 20 years. This requires you to make a lifetime commitment. Some macaws are even known to live up to the age of 50-60 years.

- **There can be considerable damage to your home:** Macaws love to chew. This is instinctive and cannot be prevented unless you provide them with enough toys and perches to chew on. Your favorite piece of furniture can be reduced to pieces in minutes. They can also make homes in your walls, clothes or lampshades. All in all, you cannot leave anything lying around with your macaw outside the cage.

- **You have to reset your lifestyle:** There are several things in the house that you cannot use anymore after you bring the macaw in. This includes scented candles, aerosols, nonstick appliances etc. You cannot leave windows open if the bird is out of the cage. They also have the habit of making loud noises at dawn and dusk. This means you will have to work on your sleep schedule as well. You will need to make arrangements to leave your bird behind whenever you have to go out of town. So last minute vacations are out of the picture.

- **They can be manipulative:** Macaws learn how to control humans. They know that a bite or a shriek is good enough to get their way. This may even happen from time to time with a parrot who is very well trained.

- **Be cautious with kids:** If you have kids in your home, make sure that you think twice before bringing a macaw home. To begin with, these birds are huge and can inflict a lot of damage when they decide to go batty. Children usually have a lot of energy and are known to make quick movements. This does not go down well with Blue Macaws. A small bite can be very dangerous for young children.

- **They can get possessive:** Macaws are known for being one human birds. They will often choose one member from the family as their human simply because they "click" with that person. However, their inherent possessiveness can pose a threat to other people. They may become aggressive when someone approaches their human. This even includes your spouse, your child or friends. Again, this behavior is also seen in birds that are well trained. That said, macaws are also known to shift loyalties. If there is someone else who has something that they want, don't be surprised if your bird decides to get friendly with them.

- **You will have to deal with hormonal changes:** Each year, your bird will reach sexual maturity two times. This is when they change quite drastically in behavior. At around the age of two, it is absolutely necessary for your bird to find a mate. That is when they become crabby and quite aggressive. They tend to lash out suddenly, bite and become extremely warning. Breeding and mating birds also requires some skills. Only when you are ready for this should you think about opening your home to a Blue Macaw.

- **They are not fond of cuddles:** Going by their looks, these birds look goofy and extremely cuddly. Of course, they are extremely gorgeous which will attract several hugs and kisses. This is not appreciated by the bird at all. Even the mates of birds only touch the head and feet of the bird. Unless your bird trusts you completely, you should never attempt to cuddle and pet him. You may also want to learn the right way to handle your macaw. Here is more stress on the point that these birds are extremely powerful. Even a friendly nip can draw blood or cause permanent damage to fingers and appendages at times.

- **Slightest negligence leads to serious behavioral issues:** The hardest part is when your Macaw becomes unhappy. If you are negligent in the care that you provide to your macaw, he will develop issues like screaming, plucking and biting. Of course, this could be seasonal because of the hormones. However, as a pet owner, you need to make sure that you don't just love your bird but respect him as well. Spending time with him, giving him a clean environment and avoiding any behavior that makes him uncomfortable are signs that you respect your pet. That is when he will truly be happy.

The advantages

Although these birds are very high maintenance, they are not all bad. The blue macaws have become popular pets with good reason. They are known to adapt wonderfully with humans. They also make loving pets who will be your companions for life. Here are a few reasons why having a blue macaw as a pet can change your life for the better:

- Having a blue macaw is very rewarding. Initially, you will feel the stress of having a macaw at home. However, the moment you forge that bond of trust with your bird, you will share the most beautiful relationship with him. He will accompany you for the smallest chores around the house, will be the perfect buddy to come home to and will be your friend for life.

- These birds are gorgeous. The feathers are colored in the most unbelievable shades of blue. They are a treat to the eyes and there is a sense of pride that comes with bringing a macaw home.

- These birds are highly complex. This means that there is never a boring moment with them around. They are very entertaining and engaging. Macaws are curious birds and will love to explore the house, learn new things from you and just play with you endlessly. It is also a treat to watch them play by themselves, often performing funny antics.

- A macaw choosing you as their human is the best compliment that you will receive in your life. The fact that a bird that is always on guard chooses to trust you is a feeling that cannot be matched.

- They are the best ice breakers. If you take your bird out for a stroll or if you have visitors in your home, you can be assured of great conversations around the bird. The beauty of these birds is one of the best ice breakers as you will always have someone who wants to get closer and get a better look.

Are apartments safe for macaws?
While macaws are generally happy if you have a large enough cage for them, you need to think about a few things when you bring your bird into an apartment, especially ones where you live in close quarters with others.

- Make sure that your neighbors are okay with the few loud shrieks that your bird is likely to let out. You can reduce the noise by keeping bird safe plants in the room of your macaw, training him well and by keeping him physically and mentally stimulated.

- Check with the local Forest and Wildlife Authorities for any licenses that are required for your pet Macaw. This is true for those living in apartments as well as those living in independent homes. If there is a license required, figure out the right process to obtain it.

- If you are living in a rented apartment, you must think about the expenses that you will have to bear with all the damage these birds are capable of inflicting. You also need to make sure that you check with your landlord before you bring the bird home. Some of them may not be comfortable with the idea of having a bird in their apartment.

- Ensure that your apartment is bird proofed. We will talk in detail about this in the following chapter. Since apartments are smaller spaces, the chances of your bird getting into things you don't want him to get into are higher. This includes the kitchen, the toilets, or even escaping out the window because the space available to him is less.

Blue Macaws are undoubtedly among the most amazing pets you can have. But if you are not responsible for them, they can be your worst nightmare.

Several birds are abandoned each year because owners are unable to keep up with the demands of having a bird at home. These birds are complex beings and not merely cage ornaments as most people consider them to be. No doubt they are gorgeous but there is so much more to them besides that.

It is hard for abandoned birds to find homes as they come with several behavioral issues that are the result of negligent ownership. If you are not sure about bringing a bird home yet, you can offer to look after a blue macaw if you know someone who has one. You can also foster a bird for a few days. Then, if you think that you are ready, you can open your home and heart to them. If not, you can simply assure yourself that you have done the right thing by deciding not bring one home.

Chapter 2: Preparing for a Blue Macaw

Macaws are large birds. You need to be prepared not only with the supplies but also with ample information about the bird that you plan to bring home. This chapter tells you everything that you need to know about being prepared for a pet Macaw.

1. Gathering information about macaws

There are several sources available for the information that you need about macaws. Here are some common sources that you can look for:

The Internet:

This is, perhaps, the best source today. It is easily accessible and is available at any time. Whether you have doubts about the species that you want to bring home or want to know about providing care for your new bird, you can look it up on the Internet. There are various bird care forums that you can join. Blogs by experts provide authentic information that you can put to use. The only issue that you will face with the Internet is the abundance of information. Some of the content may also be misleading.

You can download e-books that are dedicated to the species of bird that you want to bring home. The information in these books is well-researched and quite reliable.

Bird clubs:

There are local bird clubs such as the Parrot Society or The Real Macaw Club whose members have a lot of information with respect to different species of Macaws. This is the most reliable source. All members are dedicated to ensuring that pet birds get the right care. There are also several Macaw owners who can give you tried and tested tips to care of your bird.

Bird clubs can also help you with legalities related to your bird. If you need any license or permissions for your bird, you can contact a local bird club for information.

Avian vets:

Avian vets are specialized veterinarians who work with birds and other exotic species. Look for an avian vet near you before you bring your bird home. We will discuss about avian vets in detail in the next section. They have a lot of updated information and are definitely the most reliable source. Finding a good avian vet will give you the best possible support to raise your bird. From the time you bring your bird home, you will be able to consult your vet about different things like feeding the bird, cleaning and providing the right environment for the bird to stay healthy.

Other bird owners

If you have friends or relatives who have birds such as macaws or even other species of parrots, they can be of great help to you. They will tell you about the challenges that you will face as a bird owner. They can also provide practical solutions for these issues.

Make sure you collect as much information as possible before you bring your bird home. If needed, you can even foster a macaw for a few days to understand your equation with these birds. Then, you can make the commitment.

2. Are you ready for a macaw?

There is a simple test that you can carry out at home before you bring a macaw home. That way you will know what to expect when the bird is actually home. Try these simple activities for a month before you make the final decision. Following that, you will know if you are really ready or not.

- Take big bite of a carrot or any other fruit or vegetable. Chew it well till it is mushy and spit it out on your wall or on the floor anywhere in the house. Then, let it dry until evening. Once it is fully dried, you will have to wipe it down. Do this every day.

- A Blue macaw is expensive. During the last two months of your exercise to prepare for your bird, go to a supply store and buy everything that you need for a macaw including food and toys. Now, buy your groceries with the remaining money. Is the money that is left over from here good enough to sustain a possible lifestyle that you have created for yourself over the years? If not, how are you going to deal with the extra expense? You cannot make any compromises as far as the requirements of the macaw goes.

- Go to a pet store near your home and place a newspaper at the floor of any large macaw cage. At the end of the day, you will have an idea about the amount of poop you will have to deal with on a daily basis. Now imagine this on your furniture, clothes, the floor etc. occasionally. Is that something you can manage?

- In a gallon box, mix up some feathers, some dried poop and bird seeds or pellets. Now, these things are available in any pet store. Tell them why you need it and they will give it to you, although slightly amused. This mixture should be thrown around the house and cleaned up at least twice every day.

- Although this may sound a little dramatic, it is worth trying. Take a screwdriver and make some holes in your wall. Not all the way through, just to look like it has been gouged by a bird. Now, look at your favorite lamp, imagine it is smashed into pieces. Practice this mental exercise every day.

You need to be well researched about the bird. Read up as many journals and blogs about the Blue macaw as possible. There are certain terms that you need to know such as cloaca, blood feather, papillae, regurgitation etc.

- Sift a cup of flour around the house. Make sure you dust all the surfaces of your home. Clean this up. Repeat this every week at least three times.

- You can get a copy of wild bird sounds that can be timed and played. Play this in the morning for fifteen minutes and at sunset for fifteen minutes. Make sure you play it at full volume.

- Pick out odd things like tissue paper, bottle caps etc. and try to make interesting toys out of them. This is a skill you will have to master as Blue macaws are easily bored with toys and need something new on a daily basis. You can, of course, not splurge on these toys every day. You will soon realize that your bank account is all over the place.

- Keep aside $100 in addition to the supplies that you just bought. This is the medical expense that you can expect. How are you financially placed after putting all this money away?

Besides this, you need to be prepared for things like walking to a grocery store with dry bird poop on your shoulder. They will also gouge holes into your upholstery and your bed sheets. Of course, your bird may also require 15-20 minutes of undivided attention on a daily basis to prevent it from getting bored and developing unwanted health issues.

You need to be sure that following this regime for six months has not driven you crazy. When you commit to a Blue macaw, you will have to do all this and a lot more for at least 25 years. That is the average lifespan of these birds.

The idea is not to scare you about Blue macaws. But, this is the truth when you bring a bird home. You could ask any bird owner and they will tell you that everything above is spot on. These exercises will also help you understand whether your entire family is ready to make a commitment to a Blue macaw or not.

Ask yourself these questions
Here are a few simple questions that you can ask yourself to know if you are truly ready for the responsibility or not:

Do you have enough time for the bird?

A lot of people look for a bird that does not need too much attention or one that is "low maintenance". If you are one of them, you must reconsider having any type of bird. They need a lot of quality time and it is better if each member in your family can spend some time with them. Only if you are willing to make that commitment should you get a Blue Macaw.

Are you prepared for the expenses?

The bird itself can cost you anything between $150-$800 or £70-500 depending upon whether you choose to adopt the bird or buy a certain hybrid. Then you have to invest in a cage that can cost between $100-$500 or £60-£200. Including other expenses such as the food, bedding, veterinary visits, toys and other supplies, you will need to shell out close to $500-600 or £200-300 per annum. Of course, this does not include any medical emergency that can just shake the whole budget up. Only when you know that you have the funds for regular and emergency expenses, should you own a macaw.

Did you know that a macaw can be very messy?

From regurgitating food, coating the beak with smashed food and shake it all around the cage or just leaving feather dander everywhere, macaws can make quite a mess. Of course, you cannot rule out the fact that they poop around the clock. Sometimes, even after the bird has been potty trained, there are chances that he will poop on your favorite clothes or on expensive upholstery. If you are very meticulous in your housekeeping, be prepared for a big mess when you bring the bird home. If you do not want a mess, you should not have a macaw.

Is the bird meant to be a gift?

When the holiday season arrives, we all get a little carried away and try to spoil our loved ones with anything that they want. But, if you are giving away a Blue Macaw as a gift, think twice. Is the other person ready for the responsibility? Are you sure that the bird fits into their schedule? Do they have financial resources to care for the bird? If you are not sure, then do not gift a Blue Macaw.

Even if you think that the person is going to be able to do all of the above, make sure that you also arrange for behavioral, nutritional and environmental counselling with a vet or with rescue facilities that have them. If your loved one is reluctant to attend these, then you have a reason to take the bird back and make sure it gets a good home.

Are you considering a pet for your child?

A macaw is not a good pet for a child. Normally, pet shops and breeders do not sell a bird to a child because of several unpleasant experiences. These birds are large and powerful. The fact is that although your child is generally very responsible and is actually saving up to buy a macaw, the bird may not be a safe bet for the child. They are easily startled and can nip in defense.

In addition to that, there is also a chance that the child may lose interest eventually. This will put all the responsibility on you. If you are unable to fulfil that, you will have a neglected bird or even worse, a bird that will eventually be abandoned.

Is the Blue Macaw meant to be a companion to another bird?

Sometimes, when we are unable to give our pets as much time as they need, the guilt makes us believe that they need a friend of their own kind. If that is the purpose of bringing a Blue Macaw home, then it is useful to know that no matter how many birds you have, they will all need time and attention from you.

Are you ready to make different kinds of foods for your macaw?

Just a bowl of birdseed in the corner of the cage is not good enough. It will lead to a lot of health and behavioral issues. When you bring a macaw home, you also take on the responsibility of chopping vegetables and fruits, making sprouts and making special pellet mixes that are nutritious for your bird. Unless you have the time for this, you should not bring a pet bird home.

Do you know that a Blue Macaw lives long?

In captivity, Blue Macaws live for at least 30 years on an average. Some live as long as 50 years. This means that there is chance that the generation after you will also have to take care of the macaw depending on how old you are when you buy one. In addition to that, do you think that you can plan that far ahead? What if your job gets more demanding or if you have to move? What about when you have a newborn in the house? Will you be able to manage your bird through all these life changes?

Each year several macaws are abandoned because their owners did not expect so much work. They deserve to be in a home where you not only prepare to bring the bird home but also prepare for the future and ensure that the bird gets a good life.

3. Preparing your family

It is not enough for you to know what it takes to have a Blue Macaw as a pet. These birds are large and can be hard to maintain if you do not handle them correctly. So, every member of your family should be prepared. This is not only to ensure safety but to also ensure that your bird gets a lot of love and affection from the entire family.

When you are bringing a blue macaw home, it is natural for the family to be just as excited as you to welcome home a new member of the family. However, the blue macaw isn't just any pet bird, it is a sizeable bird with great mandible power and several special requirements.

This bird is also highly sensitive and will analyze every situation in your home before becoming a part of the household. So, you need to lay a few ground rules to prepare your family for the bird as well:

- The bird will not be disturbed during its initial days in your home. This includes no teasing, no bringing friends over to see the bird, no parties, no loud music and even no talking to the bird. That way, you can establish a sense of security with the new members.

- One must never stick their finger into the cage even for fun. These birds will bite when threatened. And, the bite will be powerful enough to rip a person's finger tip off.

- The responsibilities of feeding the bird will be divided. Initially, the other family members can be accompanied by the person whose bird it is. Then, they will have to do this on their own. Spending time feeding the bird, especially, helps the bird know all the members of the family and associate them with food which is quite positive. Birds are not threatened by their family or their flock as long as they are part of the daily routine.

- Everybody will learn about the blue macaw in complete detail. They can also attend the basic training class with you if you are adopting your bird.

- No one will tease the bird with large and colorful objects like balls or toys. These things make the bird look at you like a predator and will withdraw himself from you. They will also make the bird susceptible to behavior issues if repeated persistently.

- Whoever leaves the house last will check all the doors and windows and will make sure that the cage is closed. If there are any other additional measures like separating the household pets, it should be done by this person. The person leaving the house last is responsible for taking all the safety measures with respect to the bird who will be left alone all day.

- Only one person in the house will take the responsibility of training the bird. If you use multiple methods or cues, the bird will simply get confused and will not respond to training effectively. This is usually done by the person who is closest to the bird or by someone who has better experience with training and caring for birds.

- Do not encourage the household pets to attack the cage even for fun. Cats or dogs are natural predators who may cause a lot of harm to your blue macaw. In the case of this large bird, even vice versa is possible, considering the size and the power of this bird.

When you bring a blue macaw home, you need to understand that you are bringing home a highly evolved life form. They understand the slightest changes in their ambience. It is the job of the entire family to ensure that they bird feels comfortable in the house and feels like a part of the flock.

Your family should be educated about the needs of blue macaws to make sure that they are alert in case of any emergency. If nothing else, you need to make sure that they know how to provide first aid for common accidents like bleeding and broken feathers.

The whole family should be aware of where the first aid box is placed and where the supplies for the birds are located. They should also have the number of the vet on their phones. This way, you are all on the same page as far as first aid and emergency care is concerned.

The larger the flock, the happier a blue macaw is. So make sure your family can be the ideal and most loving flock imaginable.

4. What do Blue Macaws eat?
The diet of your blue macaw is of utmost importance. You need to make sure that you have some food ready for your macaw before you bring him home.

If you are bringing a macaw home from a breeder or a pet store here are a few things to keep in mind:

- Do not introduce any new diet to the bird all of a sudden. If the bird has been on a purely seed diet, you can introduce new food in small portions and slowly eliminate seed from the bird's diet.

- You can ask for some feed from the breeder or the pet store. Familiar food is easier for the bird to digest. Making a transition is hard for macaws. The more familiar things you have around, the easier it becomes.

- Ask about any specific allergies that the bird may have. If the bird has any allergies, also consult the vet before you make any changes to the diet.

Natural diet of blue macaws
In order to provide the right food, you need to understand their natural diet. The diet of blue macaws is very specific. This is because they come from a region of the world that has certain exotic species of plants that make up their diet.

The way these birds consume their food is also quite different. They have a specific way of easing the process of digestion. These birds generally eat palm nuts as a major part of their diet. They acquire the nuts by harvesting them from the trees. But to make it easy to digest, they forage the dung of cattle. The dung consists of just the nut which cattle cannot digest. The fibrous outer cover is digested completely. That way, the bird has very little work to do!

One thing you need to remember about the diet of blue macaws is that the diet should be rich in fat. They are able to digest fat very easily. They will not eat anything else, in fact. To feed them only fresh produce such as fruits and veggies takes a good amount of effort from your end.

What to feed them
The diet should consist of a base of pellets and seeds along with a lot of fresh fruits and vegetables. Since palm nuts are not available easily, you can also think of giving your bird walnuts, almonds, Brazil nuts, coconut, cashews, pistachio and macadamia nuts.

Commercial food pellets and treats such as Nutri-Berries, Avi-cakes and others fulfil the nutritional requirements of your blue macaw. You can encourage the foraging habit of your macaw with these foods as well.

There is a feeding routine that you need to maintain with your blue macaw. We will talk about that in greater detail in the following chapters. When you bring your bird home, make sure you at least have some seeds and pellets ready. Having some treats handy will help you gain your bird's trust.

5. Keeping the housing area ready

Don't wait for the bird to come home to set the housing area up. Although you may have a temporary carrier in place when you bring the bird home from the breeder or the pet store, try to move him into the permanent housing area the day you bring him home.

That way, you will give your bird all the time to settle down. Changing cages in the midst of his settling down process adds to the stress that he is already experiencing.

The housing area is where your bird is going to spend most of his time. So, you need to make sure that it is perfect. There are a few things that you need to think about when you set up the housing area:

- The size of the cage
- The material used to build it
- The type of cage
- The placement of the cage
- The accessories that you put into the cage

Cage size

Blue Macaws are large birds. Nevertheless, they need to have enough space to flap around and even fly a little in the housing area. You need to make sure that the bird is able to spread his wings in all directions when he is in the cage. The minimum size of the cage is 42X42X72 for the bird to feel comfortable in it.

Remember that your bird may spend the whole day in the cage or at least 12 hours every day. So, making sure that the cage is safe is a must.

If you are able to get a cage that is double the recommended size, it is called a true flight cage. This means that the bird is actually able to fly in this cage. You must also be able to fit in perches in the cage without getting in the way of the bird.

If the cage is way too small, there can be unwanted injuries when the bird flaps his wings. The feathers or the wings will get caught in the bars, leading to broken feathers and wings.

Cage material

Macaws are extremely powerful birds. If you do not get a strong enough cage, it will lead to escapes. The best material for a blue macaw cage is stainless steel. These cages are a lot more expensive than the powder coated ones.

However, the ease with which the birds can bend the bars of any other material makes it worth spending the money. You could consider it a onetime investment. Any other material will be destroyed in just a few weeks of putting the bird in.

With stainless steel you can also avoid the problem of peeling paint. As the birds climb the cage, they may peel the paint off and even ingest it. Even if the paint is said to be lead free, you need to make sure that the flakes or the chunks of paint will not cause any internal damage to the bird. The best thing is to avoid any cage or housing that contains paint.

Cage Style

There are several types of cages that are available to you. Some are ornamental while others are practical. In the case of blue macaws, the best options include the dome top cage and the play top cage. The dome top cage is popular because there is a lot of space available inside for you to add accessories like perches.

In the case of the play top cages, you have a flat surface on top that becomes a great playing area for the birds. This gives your bird ample room outdoors to play and have a good time.

When you buy a cage for your blue macaw, you also need to check things like the lock on the doors, the distance between the bars, the thickness of the bars etc. If the cage has horizontal bars, it makes climbing a lot easier. Now, you also need to make sure that the bars have been welded into place to ensure that they are sturdy.

Cage placement

The cage must occupy a quiet area in your home that is free from movements of people. There should be ample, yet not harsh sunlight. The cage that you place the macaw in should be away from the main road or noisy streets that may startle the bird. The best place would be one of the rooms in your home where the cage is placed against a wall for the bird to feel comfortable and secure. The bird should be able to watch you from this area but should not be in the middle of your activity.

Cage accessories

It is the accessories that complete the cage set up. If you just have an empty cage, you will not be successful in creating any positive associations that will make the bird want to go back into the cage. You need several accessories like toys and perches that will make the cage a rather interesting place for the bird to be in. This will come in very handy when you begin to train the bird. So, make sure the following accessories are included:

- **Toys:** Toys are the most important accessories to ensure that the bird is mentally stimulated. There are different kinds of toys that you can opt for including climbing toys, chewing toys and foraging toys. Each one offers a different kind of experience for your bird.

  When choosing these toys, make sure that they are free from small parts that could be swallowed by the bird. You also need to make sure that the material used does not consist of any toxins in the paint or the material of construction. Only use good quality toys inside the cage of your bird.

  Lastly, when you are hanging the toys, avoid using wires and strings. The bird may get tangled in these wires or threads, leading to cuts and even choking. You will get bird safe hooks with most of the good quality toys. You can also use a safer alternative which is steel chains. These are sturdy and are suitable to even hold up the perch which will carry the entire weight of the large blue macaw. With this bird, you need to be sure that all suspended items are sturdy to prevent falls and injuries.

- **Perches:** A proper perch is a must for your bird to have a good resting area. You can put up store bought perches that are available in several sizes and colors or may even make a perch out of wood yourself. If you are using a twig or piece of wood as the perch, make sure that the material is free from the poop of any wild bird. That way, you can be assured that the bird will not develop infections or other diseases.

For birds, it is very important for them to be able to trust the perching area. If it breaks or if the bird has any accident while on the perch, he will simply never get back on the perch again. That is why you need to make sure that it is hung up with good quality chains or hooks. These chains should be safe and should not have any sharp ends that may hurt the bird.

- **Food and water bowls:** Of course, your cage is incomplete without these two important elements. You need to have food and water bowls that are easy for the bird to eat or drink from. At the same time, they should be free from any toxic elements like lead or zinc.

It is recommended that you use only stainless steel or porcelain bowls for your bird cage. These materials are not damaged easily and are also very easy to clean. Do not buy any bowl with intricate design elements as they will be harder to clean and may have left overs of fruit and vegetables that can make your bird very unwell.

Place these food and water bowls near the door of the cage. This will make it much easier for you to access them. This placement will also be very useful when you are training your bird to go in and out of the cage.

- **The substrate:** Birds are pooping machines. On average, your blue macaw will poop every 15 minutes. Therefore, you need to line the cage with material that is absorbent enough and safe for the bird at the same time.

The best option is layers of newspaper, although it is debated that the ink in the paper can be hazardous to the bird's health. Choose matte finish papers without too many pictures to address this issue. You must never use wood shavings as the bird may develop several health issues due to damp wood. It is a good idea to place a grate on the floor of the cage to make sure that your bird is not walking all over his own poop.

You can add additional elements such as a sleeping tent to make your cage look more attractive. Of course, people like to add colorful toys and ribbons as well to make the cage seem more ornamental. In any case, the simpler the better as your bird will also be safe while the cage is complete with all the basic elements in it. You can get creative and change the interiors from time to time.

6. If you have other pets at home

One very important consideration is if you have other pets, especially birds at home. You need to be very careful to prevent any accidents related to dominance, any diseases from spreading from one pet to the other and of course, any signs of jealousy towards the new member of the family.

Your new bird and existing pet birds

The first and most important thing is to quarantine your new bird. He should be kept in a separate room entirely for at least 30 days. This will allow you to check for any health issues. Even if the bird is a carrier, you will be able to prevent any disease spreading throughout the flock with proper quarantining measures.

When you have quarantined the bird, make sure that you do not interact with the other birds after you have interacted with him. This means that the existing flock should be fed and cleaned first. If you must interact with the existing flock after you have spent time with the quarantined bird, make sure that you wash your hands thoroughly.

Introduce the birds one after the other after the quarantine period is over. Start with the bird who is the calmest of the lot. Place him and the new bird in separate carriers, next to each other. You can let them out and observe the behavior when you are around to supervise.

If there is an aggressive response, try again. If not put the birds back in and then keep them with each other for a few days. Repeat this with all the birds in the cage so they are familiar with each other.

Once this is done, put the birds in the cage together and let them be. Unless you see any aggressive behavior, you can let the birds be. Small squabbles are natural as the flock is simply establishing a pecking order among them.

Remember that with any bird, making introductions during the bluffing phase is not a good idea. It will lead to some nasty fights. Younger birds are easiest to introduce to the flock as they will not be perceived as a threat.

Your new bird and other pets
Cats and dogs are predators by the natural order. That already makes them a threat to your blue macaw irrespective of how sweet and friendly they are towards people.

During the first few days, allow the bird to become aware of the presence of the other animal. Let him watch and observe your pet cat or dog. There must be no surprises later on. Just make sure that your dog or cat does not approach the cage while you are away. Your cat, especially, should not be allowed to climb over the cage.

When the bird seems settled in, it is time for the introductions. While keeping the bird in the cage, you will let the dog or cat around it. Let them sniff and explore. If your dog begins to bark or if your cat becomes aggressive, separate them instantly.

Now, keep doing this until your dog or cat is used to the bird. That will make them ignore the new member of the family even when in the same room. When you have reached this stage, it may be safe to let the bird out and interact with the pets

You can take this liberty only when your dog or cat has been trained well to heel. When these animals are trained, the risk to the bird is reduced to a large extent as you will be able to control your cat or dog even if they just get too excited.

If you see that your pet cat or dog is chasing the bird around, you must put the bird back in the cage. In case your bird is not hand trained, wrap a towel around his body and your hands while handling him.

In any case, it is never advisable to leave the bird alone with your pets. While they may seem to get along with each other perfectly well in your presence, do not take any risks.

A dog can seriously harm the macaw with a simple friendly nibble. At the same time, a macaw is powerful enough to rip the dog's ear right off when provoked. As for cats, the biggest threat is the saliva of the cat which is poisonous for any bird.

Remember that you are dealing with highly instinctive creatures. You can never be sure of when their instinctive behavior will kick in. So, it is best that you let them interact in your presence. In case there are any signs of aggression, it is best to keep your blue macaw confined in the presence of the cat or the dog.

7. Bird proofing

Making your home safe for the bird should be your priority. There are several household items that can pose a threat to your pet bird. Although good training can avoid many accidents, you can never be too sure. Before your bird is brought home, a few mandatory bird proofing measures must be taken.

- Make sure that the cage is not placed on a hard surface. Should your bird have a fall, he can sustain serious injuries.

- The windows should be marked or should have any safe object hanging in front of it. That way, you will not have any instance of the bird flying into the windows and hurting himself.

- Electrical wires should be enclosed completely. There should not be any loose wires near the cage, especially on the floor. If someone accidentally trips on it and tips the cage over, it can be bad news for your bird.

- All the toilet lids and any water container in your home should be covered. There have been several reports of blue macaws and other species of parrot drowning accidentally.

- The cage should be away from the kitchen. There are fumes, especially those released by Teflon pans, which can be toxic for your bird. Prolonged exposure to these fumes can cause serious health issues.

- It is best to have a kitchen with a door that can be closed every time the bird is out of the cage. Hot stove tops and utensils are the number one cause of injuries in birds.

- Do not have doors that can close automatically. There are chances that your bird will get caught in between when the door is shutting.

- Table fans should be kept out of the bird's way. Make sure that all fans, table or ceiling, are off when your bird is let out of the cage.

- Always check doors and windows when you leave your home. You do not want your bird to get away if you leave the house with one of them open.

- Make sure you check if a certain plant is toxic to your bird or not when you place it near the cage of the bird.

- The cage doors should have a secure lock. A simple latch does not hold a macaw back as they will soon figure out how to let themselves out. Do not forget that you are dealing with a very intelligent bird. They are also powerful enough to just rip the lock apart.

The safer the environment, the less stressed your bird will be. You will also not have to worry about untoward incidents that will leave your bird with serious injuries. Even after all the precautions have been taken, make sure that you never leave the bird out of his cage without proper supervision.

Chapter 3: Getting the Blue Macaw to Settle

The transition from the breeder's or the pet store to your home is often stressful for the blue macaw. These birds have extremely high cognitive abilities that makes them analyze their environment closely. They also tend to form strong bonds with humans that care for them.

So, in bird terms, you are taking the blue macaw from one flock and reintroducing him to a new one. That can take some time and effort. Sometimes, birds adjust almost instantaneously.

This chapter talks about the various sources from which you can obtain a blue macaw. It also helps you understand the different transport options of the bird and methods to help the bird settle into your home.

1. Pet store or breeder?

These are the two most common sources of finding a pet bird. With the rarer species like the Glaucous Macaw, a breeder is probably a better choice. There are specialized breeders who work with certain species of birds. They are usually better with the breeding techniques and will also know about the specific care that these birds require.

Of course, there are pet stores that have exotic species, too. However, you need to be certain that they have the license required to sell exotic birds. If not you could be party to illegal pet trade that can have serious consequences.

That said, how do you know which one is better? A pet store or a breeder?

Here is a quick comparison of the two:

For those who are looking for convenience, the pet store can seem like the perfect option when it comes to buying a bird. While that is certainly an option, you must make sure that the pet store endorses good care and ethical breeding of the birds. When you are looking for a macaw in a pet store, make sure that you look for the following:

• Clean cages

- Well maintained birds
- Hygienic bird rooms that are away from the other animals being sold.
- Clean food bowls and clean drinking water for the birds.
- Knowledgeable staff
- Adequate quarantining of all the birds

It is true that breeders are hard to find because they usually live in areas that are on the outskirts or because they do not invest much in advertising. That said, there are several websites that will list reputable breeders in your vicinity. You can also look for recommendations from other parrot owners or from a veterinarian in your locality.

If you are choosing a breeder from the Internet, especially, make sure that you visit their facility before you make any commitment. In any case, you must make sure you inspect the breeding conditions before you bring your bird home to avoid nasty surprises. There are a few advantages of seeking out a blue macaw breeder:

- You will be able to actually see the conditions and the environment that the birds are raised in.

- You will be able to see the parents of the bird to rule out any chances of genetic issues.

- With most reputable breeders, you will be able to find a lot of information and support with respect to raising your birds.

It is always an advantage to buy your bird from a breeder because, unlike a pet store, the birds do not come in in large lots from different facilities. When various birds from various locations are caged together, chances are that the risk of disease is very high. Breeders are also less expensive because they usually do not have to invest in large spaces, advertising and in hiring employees for their facility. This saving is passed on to those who buy from them.

Red flags when buying from a breeder or pet store:
If you see any of the following practices with respect to the blue macaws, you need to choose a different source. You can also report these practices to the Forest Authority or any Animal Welfare authority as they are signs that the source is involved in illegal practices of pet trade:

- The bird is carried upside down or is the feet are tied when he is being transported.

- The birds are not placed in accordance to the species. Every species should be kept separately with the right labels outside the display area.

- Any band that is being used to identify the bird is not placed correctly and is causing trauma.

- Predator species are not kept far apart from the birds. This may lead to behavioral issues in the bird that you will have to deal with later on.

How to identify a good breeder?

When there is a demand for a certain breed of bird or animal, you will naturally see a rise in the number of people breeding them. While some of them are genuinely concerned about the welfare of their birds, there are others who are involved in it only for the commercial benefit. The latter may resort to unethical practices to increase the number of birds that are produced in each breeding season.

Today, with the Internet providing free advertising, there are several breeders who are listed when you look for one in your vicinity. You will probably find several websites that will show up with the name and location. It is best that you visit the aviary before you fall for cheap discounts or sales online.

Here are a few tips that will help you find a good breeder to buy your pet from:

- The breeder should have clean aviaries which are not rusty and shabby.

- The food and water bowls should not have any bird feces in them.

- The birds must not have ruffled feathers or any deformities.

- Proper quarantining measures should be taken for any bird that is sick or suspected of carrying any illness.

- When you approach a bird, he should be curious. If he sticks to a corner on the floor of the cage, he is probably unwell.

- The breeder should be willing to answer all your queries with respect to the blue macaw.

- A closed aviary system where birds from other flocks are restricted alone is a good option. The aviaries also insist that you wash your hands thoroughly or change your boots before you enter the premises where the birds are kept. This is the best option as the risk of illness is very low.

You can look for recommendations from previous clients of the breeder if possible. A good breeder will also help you meet the birds that have been bought from him. If you want to look for as many options as possible, you can sign up for email lists and groups such as "abird4sale" which is quite popular in Canada with over 800 members. You can join these groups on popular online groups such as Yahoo groups. Through these groups, you can read testimonials, get newsletters and also online magazines that will help you find the perfect breeder to source a healthy blue macaw from.

How to identify a good pet store?
If you are convinced that a local pet store is known for the quality of blue macaws that they sell, here are a few things that you need to keep in mind:

- Make sure that the pet store has a license to sell exotic birds. You can check the CITES website for all the details on the license required to buy and sell exotic birds.

- You need to ensure that these birds are being sourced by local breeders. Since importing these birds is illegal, these birds should be bred in captivity. Find out about the breeder that they deal with in detail.

- Check the ambience that the bird is being raised in. A macaw is not a commodity that you pick off the shelf even if it is in a slightly messy environment. These birds hate crammed and dirty places. They will develop behavioral problems and could also be carriers of several diseases when kept in such conditions.

- The pet store should provide a health guarantee for the birds that they sell, especially the exotic ones. Insist on this guarantee because blue macaws are extremely expensive.

- The bird should look healthy and active. On the other hand, if he or she is lethargic and is afraid of people, it might be a challenge for you to make the bird a part of your family.

- The staff should be interested in the well-being of the bird and should be able to provide you with information regarding the care and maintenance of the bird. If you see that they are negligent and are only trying to make a sale, they have most likely invested almost nothing in the bird's well-being.

What are leg bands?

With most breeders, a leg band is used to identify the bird that they are selling. These leg bands will help you get an accurate history of the bird that you are purchasing. Leg bands will also tell you how old the bird exactly is.

It is a good idea to look for breeders who will provide leg bands as you will get a lot of information about your bird. In case the bird does have a leg band, the type of leg band is necessary for you to identify so that you know what information is provided on them.

There are usually two types of leg bands:

Open bands

These bands can also be used on adult birds as they come with a clamp that closes them. There are two types of these bands. The first one is the European design which is made of aluminum. It has a cross section that is rectangular and comes with a pin that holds it together.

The European band signifies that the bird was either bred in some European country or that it is meant for export. It can also mean that a bird that was caught in the wild was sent to Europe and then put up for export. With this band, the information that you get is limited as you cannot figure out the age or the exact origin of the bird in question.

There is another type of band that comes with a cross section that is circular. These bands are mostly made of steel and are issued by the USDA for imported birds that are meant to be quarantined. They are also used by veterinarians to denote the gender of the bird after the sexing process.

With the quarantine bands you will see that there is a 3 number code that is preceded by a 3 letter code. The first letter denotes the state that the bird was imported into. These bands are usually applied when a large shipment of blue macaws is involved. These bands should fit every bird that has been sent in with the shipment. Therefore they are made larger in size. In most cases, the bands many not be closed near the seam because they were too small to fit the birds legs.

Previously, these import bands were removed by vets as they could endanger the bird. The split end is easily caught in the toys, cage bars or the rope and thread used in the cage. This makes the bird thrash around and even break his leg in the process. During that time, after the bird had been imported properly, there was no need to keep the band on.

Today, however, banding is mandatory to safely transport the birds across the borders of state. Unless the safety of the bird is compromised, you cannot remove these bands.

When used for sexing, an open band is placed on the left leg in case of females and on the right leg in case of males. When these bands were used by vets, the number of letters were different, usually 2 or 4 to help one distinguish between the import band and the sexing bands.

Sexing bands are used by professionals, therefore, they are the perfect size depending upon the bird that they are sexing. These bands will be closed properly at the split. Any band that does not close properly is probably not valid or authentic. Some breeders may just take the band off one bird's leg and put it on another to make you believe that surgical testing has been done.

Closed bands

These bands are also called breeder bands or seamless bands because they are used on captive bred birds. They are placed on the feet of baby birds. They are flat and come with a cross section that is rectangular.

For this band to fit properly, it needs to be used on baby birds before their eyes are open. That is when it will slide into place comfortably. On an average the bird will be between 10 and 14 days of age when this band is put on them. So they cannot be smuggled easily.

You have a number-letter code and also the year when it was applied and the country or the province that the birds were born in. There are different colors to signify the age of the bird with just one glance.

If a breeder is part of a club, the name of the club is engraved on it as well. Some clubs will use a logo or symbol. You can trace these bands back by contacting any local breeder.

If the band is sourced form a particular company, it is harder to trace but it can be personalized as the breeder wants.

There are very rare instances of closed bands that are not authentic. You will sometimes find that the band is so large that you can just squeeze it right off the foot of the adult bird. The codes are also suspicious with just some number and no other information. These breeders do not want their aviary to be identified. The reasons for this are quite obvious.

Of course, there are several cases when the birds are bred perfectly but are not banded. This is when the breeder is simply unaware of the advantage of banding. The breeder is probably a newcomer who has been unable to source the bands. They may have also missed the right age to band the babies after which the foot is just too large.

Some breeders just do not believe in banding as they consider it harmful to the bird. However, no instance of injury has ever been reported due to a breeder band. If possible, get a baby who has a band on his leg. In case he is not banded, you can ask the breeder why that happened and can also ask to meet the clutch from which the bird has been picked. If all the birds are healthy, then your bird is also in good condition.

Is the bird healthy?
With younger birds, the signs of diseases are very mild and almost absent. This makes it extremely hard to know if you are bringing home a healthy bird or not. In fact, blue macaws hide illnesses very well even when they are older. If you are observant, you will be able to find a few warning signs that could imply that the bird is unwell or has some abnormalities. These signs include:

The condition of the feathers

If you are handed a small, fluffy baby bird, it does seem cute and you may even believe that it is how they are supposed to look. However, by the time a baby blue macaw has been weaned, he is practically the size of an adult. The bird is able to perch like an adult and also has fully developed feathers.

A bird that has feathers that seem disheveled when they are younger, it is quite normal as baby birds tend to be hard on their plumes. However, the down feathers should not stick out in between the colored feathers and through them. This is a sign that the bird is plucking his feathers or that the parents are doing so.

Bad plumage is also a sign that the bird has been weaned too early or has some disease. There are several serious illnesses in case of macaws that will affect the feathers.

The activity level

If you notice that the bird is in a corner of the cage and continues to sleep even if you approach him, he is probably unwell. It is true that young birds sleep a lot more than adults. However, with anything that is interesting such as a new visitor, they will become alert. If you are unsure, visit the bird a couple of times more to see if the activity level improves.

Appearance of nostrils and eyes

In birds, infections ted to manifest in the form of an eye infection or a plugged nose or blocked sinus. If you notice that the eyes are cloudy or red or that the nostrils have some discharge, it is a definite sign of illness. If the infection is minor, it can be cured with simple medication. However, it is best that you wait for at least a week to check on the bird. You must ensure that this bird is quarantined even if he seems like he is in perfect health when you buy him.

The weight of the bird

The bird that you are planning to buy should neither be overweight, nor should it be undernourished. The keel bone, which is present near the belly, just above the bird's legs is a good indicator of the body condition of the bird.

In adult birds, the bone should be in line with flesh and must not protrude. In the case of baby birds, it tends to protrude a little after they have been weaned because they are usually active and also because they may lose some weight after weaning. If you notice that the bone is jutting out by more than $1/8^{th}$ of an inch, the bird still needs to develop before you take him home. In the case of an adult bird, that is a sign that the bird is malnourished and that he may also have underlying health issues.

Even when you are certain that your bird is healthy, make sure that you get a health guarantee. You see, in birds, it is hard to tell if they are healthy or not immediately. Should you notice any issues after the purchase, a health guarantee will be useful.

What you must look for
There are a few things that are advantageous for bird owners to make sure that their birds are a perfect fit for their home. When you are buying a bird from a breeder or a pet store, here are a few things that you can look for:

Are the birds hand-raised?

Not too long ago, finding birds that were hand raised was not easy. You could probably find them with breeders, but not really in pet stores. Today, the picture is quite different with hand raised birds being the preferred choice. Even in pet stores, they are hand raised to make them tamer and more social when it comes to human beings.

Hand raised birds are those that have been removed when they are hatchlings and then raised by human beings. Some breeders and pet stores will co-parent with the parent birds, but the babies are not raised entirely by the parents.

This makes the bird people oriented. That way, you have a "pet" from the time the bird enters your home. The bird will probably even step up on your finger or arm without much hesitation. These birds are less likely to bite as well. They do not perceive you or your hand as a threat.

When you visit a breeder, make sure that you ask for birds that are hand tamed, unless you are willing to spend the time it requires to train the bird and make him tame. Breeders will not hand raise a bird most often because they do not have the time and the resources required. In most cases, these birds are shipped off to pet stores and are sold at much lower costs than one that is hand tamed.

You will pay a price for this with a bird that may not become as tame as you want it to be. It is possible to make them social, but it requires careful training and probably a few nips from time to time.

When you pick a bird that you want to take home, it is a good idea to insist that you handle it. Even with birds that have been hand raised, particularly with blue macaws that have a tendency to bluff, you will find them becoming nippy or skittish around people. This is a sign that the birds are not being hand tamed.

With most places, the bird will be handled only when he needs assistance to eat. Once the bird has been weaned, he will be left in the aviary with the other birds with very little human interaction. These birds are more oriented towards birds, in comparison to people. These birds will most often try to bite when you reach out for them.

Birds that have been weaned correctly and trained to be easy to handle will, no doubt, be more expensive. This is because of the effort involved in making them that way.

The younger you can buy your bird, the better it is. That way, you will not only have a hand fed bird, but you can also make sure that he gets the attention that he needs after he has been weaned. Younger birds also adapt a lot faster than older ones.

Should the bird be weaned?

Most avian experts and experienced pet owners will discourage you from buying a bird that has not been weaned. The period of weaning can be really stressful on the babies and if you try to move them in that time, it gets even worse.

Research with popular veterinary facilities reveals that birds that have been sold or moved just before they are weaned are at a higher risk of developing health issues. This risk is greater if you already have pet birds at home and you have to introduce the new one to them. This is because the immune system is compromised with stress. It is true that birds that have already been weaned and are capable of feeding on their own are stronger in terms of immunity.

If you are new to the world of macaws, hand feeding is not very easy. It is also risky. Even if you know of people who have been successful at doing so, it is best not to take a chance. It depends on the personality of the bird and each bird is different when it comes to hand feeding. Some are easier than others.

There is also a room for a lot of error when you are new. For instance, the formula may be a little overheated. This can cause serious crop issues and irritation in the crop lining. As a result, the bird may develop many infections. This damage happens very fast between the time the baby has stopped eating and the food stops moving through the crop. You need some experience to recognize a possible problem.

If you have a breeder or a pet store trying really hard to sell you a baby bird that has not been weaned, they are possibly trying to save themselves from the trouble. This is passed on to you along with a lot of risk to the well-being of the bird.

You will hear a lot of reasons like the bonding between you and your bird will be better or than he will love you more. In the wild, birds do not form permanent bonds unless they reach adulthood and have reached the breeding age. In the case of blue macaws, the fact that they are not monogamous also leaves you a lot of room to bond with your pet.

All you need to do is be willing to give the bird the time, train him, make sure that you feed him well and keep him healthy in order to form a strong bond. Macaws will form a strong bond with one owner in most cases but are a lot easier to adapt in comparison to any other parrot breed.

When you handle your potential pet bird, here are a few things you need to look for additionally:

Does the bird only show a strong bond for one person?

If the breeder is able to bond with the bird and not anyone else from the family, say his wife, then there are chances that the bird will show a dislike for women in general. This behavior can be altered if you have the time for it. If not, you might want to look for a bird that is capable of bonding with others while maintaining one strong bond with one human. That is the safer option if you want to prevent accidents.

Is the bird prone to screaming or biting?

Very often, birds pick up bad behavior because people, unknowingly, reinforce them. For instance, giving the bird a treat to stop screaming or even giving him attention is a sign for the bird that this is acceptable to behave in that manner. While they pick these behavior patterns easily, it can be really hard to get rid of them.

You may notice that the bird is calm in the presence of new people but will soon show this behavior when he has adjusted to their presence. This is why it is best that you spend some time with your potential bird before buying one.

Remember, once you have brought the bird home, you need to even out any behavior quirks. They are certainly changeable. With some birds it may take a few days while with others it can take several months or even years. If that is the type of commitment you are willing to make, then consider a pet macaw. This can hamper your relationship with the bird if you are not willing to work on it.

How old is the bird?

This is a really important question for you to ask. With store bought birds, you may not be able to know the exact age, but an approximation at the very least is necessary. With older birds, training them is definitely more challenging. With birds that are too young, you will have to make additional efforts to keep them healthy while the immune system builds to its full capacity. A young, weaned bird is best when you are not very experienced with macaws or if you do not have enough time.

Why ask for a health guarantee?
With a reputable breeder, a health guarantee is provided with every specimen that they sell. If the seller has a health guarantee, it is an indication of good breeding practice.

With birds, it is always reasonable to believe that the bird may not be in the best of his health when you make a purchase. Should you have to return the bird, a health guarantee ensures that you get a full refund. It is best that you avoid breeders who do not provide a health guarantee.

Without a health guarantee, it is almost impossible for a buyer to prove that the breeder knew about the illness when he made a sale. With a written health guarantee, you can make up for this lack of legal protection on part of the buyer.

A health guarantee works both ways. It protects a seller if the new owner is negligent. It also helps the buyer in case the breeder did not disclose any disease that the bird could be carrying. There are a few conditions that every health guarantee contains:

- The health of your bird is guaranteed for a total of three days as long as the bird has been thoroughly examined by a certified Avian Vet. This is an expense that you need to take care of.

   Should the veterinary find any issues that makes the health of the bird unsatisfactory, you need written documentation that will state the issues.

   You must return the bird immediately for a full refund. The species and the band number of the bird must be mentioned in the document provided. The breeder will not reimburse the vet fees or any expense that you have to bear for transportation.

- In case the bird dies within 12 days of purchase, you need to make sure that a necropsy is conducted within 72 hours after the death of the bird. If you are not able to conduct the necropsy immediately, the body must be refrigerated until the tests are conducted.

   The reports of the necropsy should be sent to the veterinarian of the breeder and must include the species and the band number. If these reports prove beyond any doubt that the bird had any health issues that originated before the purchase, you will be able to get a full reimbursement or a replacement.

   Some breeders will also allow you a 6 month window during which a death of the bird will ensure reimbursement provided a proper necropsy is conducted.

   The breeder will not be held responsible for any expenses that you have to bear for these tests. You will also not hold the breeder liable if any bird from your existing flock develops any problem. It is mandatory to quarantine every new bird and if you do not do so, you cannot hold the breeder responsible.

- You must ensure that the bird has been quarantined adequately when you bring him home. He should be kept away from the other birds for at least 30 days before introducing him into the flock.

- If you already have other birds at home for a year or more, you will have to provide all the medical records of the bird and correct documentation for their health. It is possible that viruses that infect birds stay in a certain environment for many hours even after the bird has recovered fully.

- Negligence on part of the owner does not make the breeder liable for any return or reimbursement. For instance, if you leave the bird in the car on a hot day or if you do not provide the bird with adequate food and care, you cannot hold the breeder responsible for any health issues or even death.

Of course, a health guarantee does not cover for any behavioral or psychological issues. It is your responsibility to make sure that you spend time with the bird to understand his behavior before you make the purchase.

2. Can you adopt a blue macaw?

If you are a slightly experienced bird owner, you are probably ready to adopt a blue macaw. What you need to know about adopting any bird is that you are probably going to find an adult bird that also has a history of abandonment or even abuse. These birds tend to be shy or aggressive depending upon the experiences that they have had in the past.

With adoption, you need to know that the birds need additional care which you will be able to provide only after you have some experience with the birds. You may also have to spend more money on the medical treatment of these blue macaws, As they are a rare species, there are several policies regarding the adoption of these birds.

Adoption agencies that work with blue macaw species are very particular about the care that the birds are going to receive. Therefore, they have two options for all the birds that come under their care. One is lifetime sanctuary where the birds are kept in the adoption center till they die. This is normally done when the bird requires that kind of attention because of some health issue that it has. In addition to that, when some people give their birds up, they request lifetime care to make sure that the bird is in good hands.

The second option is when the birds are put up for adoption. Now, with blue macaws, they are exceptionally careful about the adoption process as these birds are highly vulnerable to exploitation for commercial gains.

The adoption process
The first step to adopting a macaw is to fill out an application form for adoption. This application form will ask for details about your profession, your experience with birds and also the reason for adoption.

Following this application form, you will be asked to take basics lessons about caring for blue macaws. These lessons could either be online or offline. You will also be given access to a lot of their educational material that you can refer to after taking the bird home. Many adoption agencies require that you complete a certain number of these basics classes before you are allowed to take a bird home.

After you have completed the required number of training hours, you will be allowed to take a tour of the aviary and the adoption center. That way, you get an idea about all the birds that are available for adoption. There are several cases when people decide that they want a certain bird but end up getting a different species altogether.

The idea is to form a bond with the right bird. Macaws are birds with large personalities. If your personality does not match the bird's personality, you will have a tough time getting your bird to bond with you and actually want to be around you.

The last thing to do would be to visit the bird of your choice frequently. Once you have made up your mind to take a certain macaw home, you need to let the bird get acquainted with you. You will also learn simple things like handling the bird, feeding him and cleaning the cage up etc. from the experts at the adoption agency.

Sometimes, it may so happen that you set your heart and mind on one bird who just does not seem to be interested. It is natural for that to happen. All you need to do is be patient with the bird and visit him as many times as you can.

When you are ready to take the bird home, most of these adoption centers will pay a visit to your home and will take care of all the little details required to help you get the bird settled into your home.

Now, if you already have pet birds at home, you will be required to present a full veterinary test result of each bird. This helps the agency ensure that the bird they are sending to your home does not have any vulnerability to fatal diseases. There are certain health standards that each of these agencies set for the health of your pet bird.

Are there any fees involved?

Most agencies and foundations will charge you an application fee that will include access to educational DVDs, toys and other assistance from the foundation.

You will also have to pay an adoption fee that may go up to $100 or £500 for a blue macaw. These two separate fees are charged to make sure that you get all the assistance that you need with respect to making a positive start with your blue macaw.

In addition to that, most agencies charge a rather high fee to ensure that the individuals who are investing in the bird are genuinely interested in having the bird. These fees will ward off people who want to just take the bird home for free with no clue about its care. Of course, you also need to consider the care provided to these birds while they are under the care of the foundation. These fees cover all of that including the medical requirements of your bird. It is also the only source to pay the dedicated staff who take care of these abandoned or rescued birds day in and day out.

From the time you make the application for a blue macaw, it takes about 6-10 weeks for it to be approved and for the bird to be sent to your home. Most of these centers will also have a probationary period of 90 days during which you will have to keep sending records of how the bird is progressing to them. They will also pay home visits to ensure that the bird is being maintained well without any health issues. If the ambience or the facilities provided to the bird are not good enough, the bird will be taken back with no reimbursement of the adoption fee.

3. Transporting your Macaw

There are different options to transport your macaw from the breeder or pet store to your home. If you are buying from a breeder who is from a different city or state, make sure that you pay at least one visit before finalizing the deal.

Depending upon where you are bringing your blue macaw from, you have the option of transporting the bird by car or by air. Here are some tips to make the travel part easier for the bird.

Driving your macaw

If this is the first time you are going to be taking the macaw in the car, there are a few things that you must take care of.

First, get the bird accustomed to the ambience of your car. Transfer him to a travel cage and place the cage in the car for a few minutes. You can leave the windows down or can turn the air conditioner on at room temperature. Never leave the bird in a hot car. In many states, this is considered illegal and is viewed as cruelty against the bird.

The next thing to do would be to get the bird used to the movement. Drive around the block and watch the bird's body language.

If he is singing and perched in an erect posture, he is quite unfazed by the movement of the car. He could even get on to the floor if the perch is shaky. But, the body language will be positive.

On the other hand, if your bird is trembling and has retreated to one corner of the cage, stop the car. Put him in his cage with lots of food and water. Try again after sometime.

As the bird gets more comfortable, you can increase the distance of your drive. Ensure that there is a lot of clean drinking water available for your bird. You must also have fresh pellets in a bowl for him to eat on the way. The substrate should be thick and have multiple layers. Your bird is likely to poop more when he is travelling.

Make sure that you stop the car every half an hour to give the bird a break. He will be able to stop, drink some water and refresh himself. On the way, keep the air-conditioner on at room temperature and keep the cage away from any drafts. Do not keep the window open as it freaks the bird out. Lastly, place the cage in the shade. Or you could put a towel over half the cage as a retreat spot for your bird. The cage should be kept in a way that prevents too much movement.

Avoid loud music. You must also avoid talking to the bird during your drive home.

Air Transport

The real challenge is when you have to transport the bird by air. Being in the cargo area at such a high altitude can be very stressful for your bird and can even lead to seizures or death when the airline is not responsible.

But before you look for airlines that will let you travel with your bird, you need to make sure that your blue macaw is allowed to enter a certain state or country. There are strict laws with respect to importing exotic parrot species in several parts of the world.

Contacting the Wildlife and Fisheries Authority in the country or state that you are travelling to will help you understand the legal considerations. You can also visit the official website of CITES to understand the laws that apply to your bird when crossing borders.

If there is any paperwork that needs to be done, make sure that you plan at least 6 months in advance. You do not want any delays to cause problems in your travel plans.

If the bird is allowed to enter a state or country, he will require a health certificate. This should be made not more than 30 days before your travel dates.

Then, contact an airline that allows pets on board. You will have to purchase a carrier that is approved by the airline. When you are ready to travel, line the carrier with enough bedding and leave a toy for your bird to have something familiar with him. Water should be provided in bottles to prevent dampness and related infections.

The airlines will be able to feed your bird at regular intervals. Of course, there is an additional service charge for this. Make sure that the cage is secured properly and the door is shut tight.

Having the bird checked within 24 hours of reaching the new home will be beneficial. There could be minor stress related health issues that can be treated easily. Even if your bird seems perfectly healthy, a good check-up is mandatory.

In most cases, the breeder will help you with all the formalities with respect to air travel. The only thing you need to make sure is that the bird is in good condition when he begins to travel. This means, you need a health certificate and a thorough report of the medical exam sent to you before the bird is transported.

4. The bird's transition into your home

Once the bird is home, it is your job to make the transition smooth for him. It is a new environment and he is likely to be scared and confused. With birds like the blue macaws that are so gorgeous, it is natural to feel the urge to pet the bird and fuss over him. But make sure you avoid this completely. Instead, follow these tips to make the transition smooth and comfortable.

Remember that every voice in your household is something entirely new for the bird. Let the bird get used to this for a few days. Placing the cage in an area that allows the bird to watch over without getting disturbed is the best thing to do.

Take the first few days to develop a routine with your bird. The first thing you will do after you wake up each morning is clean out the food and water bowls and feed your bird. You can spend some time with your hands on the sides of the cage while the bird is feeding. Make sure you are at eye level.

After a few days, the curious blue macaw will try to peck at your hand and just get a feel of what it is. Don't force it upon the bird. Let him come to you instead of the other way around.

Then get on with your chores. Make sure your bird is able to see you. When you enter the room that the bird is placed in just greet him with a hello and say goodbye when you leave the room. This should be practiced by everyone in the family so that the bird gets acquainted with the voice.

For the first few days, do not allow anyone else to feed the bird. This should be done by the person who brought the bird home. When your bird forms a bond with you, it is safer to introduce him to the other members in your family.

Lastly, the first few days are very crucial to determine if your bird is showing signs of any behavioral or physical problems. So, observe the bird carefully. If you see that there is any change from what is normal such as too much water consumption, lack of energy, staggering while walking, heavy breathing, lack of appetite or even excessive aggression, it might be a good idea to consult the vet. That way, any problem can be fixed in the initial stages so that you can enjoy the rest of your journey with your blue macaw.

Chapter 4: Your Relationship with your Blue Macaw

Building a relationship with your blue macaw takes some time and understanding. One of the basic foundations of your relationship is trust. Start with basic training to get your bird to trust you and learn to interact with you. You will also be able to understand your bird's body language as you interact with each other.

Remember to take it slow and ease into it. You can build a strong bond only with consistency and patience.

1. Training your Blue Macaw

Blue macaws are highly intelligent birds. They respond to training positively and can learn a lot of new tricks. Training your blue macaw is not only a great way to bond with him but will also keep him mentally active.

There are some basic things that you must teach your macaw to make sure that they are comfortable being handle as well. The only rule with bird training is to stay consistent and to shower him with positive reinforcement to make him respond better.

Step up training

Teaching your macaw to step up on your finger or on a perch makes him more hand tamed. Besides that, a bird who will willingly step up is easier to rescue from an unsavory situation such as a fight with a household pet or even an accident such as a fire in the house. Here are a few simple steps to begin step up training with your bird.

- If your bird is hand tamed, you can expect him to step up right away. If not, you have to first make him comfortable enough to approach your hand.

- Holding a treat through the cage bars is the first step. Then you can work your way towards opening the door and using the treat to lure the bird out of the cage.

- When the bird is comfortable with approaching you, you can hold out your finger like a perch or use an actual one.

- Then, hold a treat just behind the perch or your finger and wait for the bird to step up voluntarily before handing it out to him. Use the cue "Up" or "Step up" every time you do so.

- Do not be surprised if the bird tries to get his beak around your finger. He is only making sure that the perch is steady. Withdrawing the hand sharply will make him lose trust.

- Once the bird has stepped up, offer the treat and then set him back in the cage with another treat or toy.

- You can slowly try to hold him on the finger or perch and get him out of the cage and walk around for a while. Remember, when you put him back, make it a positive experience by providing treats.

- You can do the same to get him to step up on your shoulder or head once he is comfortable.

- Eventually, the bird will respond to the cue and will not require a treat in order to step up.

Potty training your bird

Just like you potty train your dog or cat, you can teach your blue macaw to "go" in a certain place. This will need you to observe how frequently he poops and be ready before he does.

- When the bird is about to poop, he will show some changes in his body language. Most often, the bird will lift his tail and will seem to push his body weight towards his vent. It will almost look like he is going to squat.

- Then, place a piece of paper below the bird and wait for him to poop. When he does so, shower him with appreciation and give him his favorite treat.

- Soon the bird will associate the piece of paper as the appropriate place to go.

- Even when the bird is out of the cage and you see him getting into the pooping position, just hold the paper out.

- With practice, your bird will look for the paper to poop on.

- Of course, there will be several accidents till your bird figures this out, be patient and let him learn what is expected from him.

The talking blue macaw

As a species, macaws are able to imitate human sounds very well. Their anatomical structure allows them to do so. Humans have a larynx above the trachea to allow speech. Macaws have a similar structure called the syrinx that is located at the base of the trachea. Both these function as voice boxes that can produce sounds similar to human sounds.

Macaws also have a tongue that allows them to manipulate the sound and make it very similar to human sounds. The difference lies in the hearing abilities. Birds do not have the same hearing abilities as humans. That is why they can only pick up certain sounds. Even so, your macaw can learn hundreds of words and remember them.

Blue macaws are known to be decent talkers. However, in comparison to other species of parrots like the Eclectus parrot, your blue macaw is likely to talk a lot less.

Birds merely mimic what we say. So repeating words and phrases before the bird is the best way to train them to talk. If you say hello every time you see the bird or "food time" every time you feed him, he will pick up on it and will say the word before you do some day. When he does, give him loads of treats and praise him abundantly.

Speaking to the bird every day and saying the words that you want him to learn in a high and excited voice will make him pick up on it. Another great idea to get your bird to learn words is to play the radio and also cartoons to him. He will pick up on words that he hears often.

You will also notice your bird mumbling these words to himself before he actually says them out loud. This is his way of practicing what he has learnt. It seems like your bird is actually chattering to himself when he is learning words.

2. Grooming your Blue Macaw

Grooming your blue macaw is not very hard. They will preen themselves and will take a bath in a water bowl that is placed in the cage and will keep themselves clean for the most part. However, a few grooming sessions with your bird will help build a strong bond between you and your bird.

Bathing your bird

Blue macaws love to take a bath. So, this should not require a lot of effort from your end. The only time you will have to give your bird a good scrub is if he gets any debris on his feathers or if he has some toxic material like paint on his feathers.

To urge your bird to get into a water bath, you can place a few spinach leaves or other greens in the water bath. When he steps into the bath, he will not only enjoy a good bath but will also have treats to go with it.

If the bird is hand tamed, you can pick him up and lower him into the water bowl, feet first. Slowly let him in and then allow him to enjoy the water.

The water should be lukewarm. Soap will only be used when there is some rigid dirty on the feathers. Use diluted baby soap and gently brush the debris off with a toothbrush. Rinse it thoroughly and make sure that there is no chemical residue on the body of the bird.

Misting the feathers with a spray bottle also helps keep your bird clean. But the spray can be disturbing to your bird. If he resists, you should stop immediately. Never spray on the face and eyes directly. It will be very uncomfortable for the bird to get any water in the nostrils and eyes.

Trimming the nails

If the nails of your bird grow too long, they will get caught in upholstery threads or in rope toys. If the bird tries to move, there are chances that he could break the nail or worse fracture the toe. This can be very painful which is why trimming the nails is necessary.

Textured perches are the best option when it comes to keeping the nail trimmed naturally. If you still see that the nail is overgrown, it should be trimmed. A very sharp end on the toenail means that it requires trimming.

To trim the nail of the bird, wrap a towel around him and hold him on your lap on his stomach. Then release one foot from under the towel. Place your finger under the toenail and gently file the nail till it does not feel sharp anymore. Repeat this on the other side to make sure that the nails are filed properly.

If your bird resists, take it easy as the toes are very delicate. You can trim one toe, let the bird rest and then move on to the next one. Make sure that the nail is not so short that it hampers the bird's ability to perch and climb.

Clipping the nail

You can clip the nails and still allow the bird to fly close to the ground. Many bird owners are not comfortable with this but if you believe that it may hamper the safety of your bird, you need to take adequate measures.

Clipping the tail can be tricky. You need to make sure that you do not get the blood feathers of the bird which can cause profuse bleeding. The primary feathers are the ones that need to be clipped. These are the three largest feathers on the wings of the bird.

Cutting about 1 cm is good enough to prevent the bird from getting a very good lift for flight. Hold the bird with a towel wrapped around him. Rest him on your thigh, face down. Then spread the feathers of one wing out while keeping the other wing under the towel.

Using a sharp pair of scissors, cut up to 1 cm off the primary feathers. Do the same on the other side, making sure that they are symmetrical. When they are not symmetrical, the bird will find it hard to maintain balance and will be unable to even stay on the perch comfortably.

Even when the bird's wings have been clipped, they should not be left outdoors without ant restraint such as a leash or a carrier. If there is a breeze that is strong enough to give him the lift he needs, he can get away.

3. Caring for the bird while you are away

Unless you are moving out permanently, you will probably not have the option of taking your blue macaw considering the legalities involved.

So, you need to make arrangements for your bird while you are away. Leaving your pet with your friends or relatives is the best option possible. If you have other members in your family, of course, there is no problem at all.

However, in some cases, when you have no one to take care of your bird while you are away, you may have to look for pet sitting services. The Pet Sitters International is an organization that you can depend upon in order to find the best pet sitting services. They have a list of independent pet sitters or pet sitter agencies that you can contact.

It is recommended that you contact local bird clubs to find pet sitters who have worked for the members before and have taken good care of the birds. Friends and family with birds can also provide good recommendations for you.

Now, when you are looking for a pet sitter, you need to conduct an interview with a couple of them till you can find someone reliable enough to leave your bird with. During the interview sessions, there are a few pointers that you need to keep in mind to find the perfect caretaker for your bird.

- Ask for the pet sitters' experience. They should have some knowledge about handling birds and taking care of them. If you see that your pet sitter is a novice, you should know that he at least has birds of his own.

- Ask them what they know about macaws and if they have taken care of these birds in the past. Blue macaws are large birds and has very specific requirements. One should know how to handle the bird at least. It is not the same as a Sun Conure or a smaller breed of parrot.

- Ask if they have birds of their own. Anyone who has their own pets will also be sensitive to the requirements of other people. They will be sensitive and will understand that you need the best care for your bird. They are also aware of basic body language and will be able to communicate better with your bird. A pet sitter is not someone who will just feed the birds and clean the cage. They are literally taking your place while you are away.

- Observe the way he or she handles the bird. If they are comfortable with the bird and are able to manage him or her well, then they are probably quite experienced. They must also be able to calm a bird down when he is excited or aggressive.

- You need to make sure that he or she is capable of handling an emergency. Ask them how they would deal with various emergency situations. If it is close to what you would do, then you can hire this individual without a second thought.

- In your absence, if they have a personal emergency, how will they deal with it? Will they be able to send in a substitute? If yes, you need to meet the person who will be substituting for your pet sitter to ensure that they are right for your bird, too.

Once you have finalized on a sitter, you need to discuss the cost and the services that he or she will provide. Make sure that you have it all in writing to prevent any confusion in the future.

Get all the contact details of your pet sitter including the phone number and email ID. You need to have access to him or her whenever you need. Make it a point to call every day to keep an eye on your bird.

Provide all the contact details of the place that you will be staying. You also need to provide emergency contact numbers of friends and family members.

Make a written routine for your sitter to follow. You must even include the number of your vet in this list. Ensure that your pet sitter knows where the food is stocked, how to clean the food bowls and the cage and also where the first aid kit is located.

The first time you leave your bird is the hardest. You will eventually get accustomed to one pet sitter who can take care of all your bird's needs. It is best to find a sitter who will stay at your place and take care of the bird. This reduces a lot of stress on the part of your macaw.

Travelling is one of the biggest points for consideration when you bring home a macaw. If you are a frequent traveler, do not bring a bird home.

When you have to take decisions like moving out of a country, think about your macaw. If your bird cannot go with you, are you willing to put him in foster care? If not, then you will have to make compromises on your travel for this. Only when you are willing to make these sacrifices should you bring a macaw home.

4. Bird Body Language

This is one of the most critical parts of owning a bird. As you interact, you will become familiar with several behavior patterns that your bird showcases.

The bird uses his whole body to show you different emotions. The more you interact with the bird, the more you will become aware of subtle signs that the bird will show. There are a few basic signs, however, that will help you begin your communication with your bird and read his response correctly.

Eyes
- The eyes of the bird will dilate depending upon the level of excitement, curiosity, anger or fear.
- This is called pinning or flashing.
- Make sure that you take the context of the environment around your bird and his general body posture in to account to understand exactly what the bird is trying to communicate with his eyes.

Wings
- The bird will flap his wings as a form of exercise in most cases.
- Flapping the wings is also a way to get your attention simply because your bird is happy to see you.
- Flapping the wing is also a sign of pain or anger. If you cannot see any stimulus for either, then the bird is probably just fluffing up his feathers.
- Drooping wings are a sign of fatigue. If the wings droop even when the bird is resting, it is a sign that your bird is unwell.

Tail

- Like any other animal, the tail is an important medium of communication.
- Wagging the tail indicates that your bird is happy.
- If he fans out his tail feathers, the bird is trying to show dominance by looking larger. This is done during the breeding season or just before he is going to attack.
- Bobbing of the tail after play and exercise indicates that the bird is just trying to catch his breath.
- Bobbing of the tail otherwise is an indication of respiratory issues.

Leg and feet
- Tapping the feet is often seen as a sign of aggression in your bird. He does this to assert dominance.
- The legs will appear weak after you have played with your bird and are putting him back in the cage. This is no cause for worry as the bird is just resisting going back in to the cage.

Beak
- Grinding of the beak shows that your bird is happy and content.
- If he clicks the beak once, he is simply greeting you and saying hello.
- Multiple clicks on the other hand are a sign of warning and it is best that you stay away from your bird.

Body posture
- If the body of the bird is erect and alert but the muscles are relaxed, it shows that he is happy.
- An alert body with stiff muscles means that the bird is showing dominance and is probably going to attack.

Vocalization
- Sounds like chattering, whistling and singing are a sing of contentment in your bird.
- Growling and purring indicates aggression or disapproval.
- Clicking of the tongue means that he wants to play with you.

These signs will become clearer as you interact with your bird. You will also see certain movements and body postures unique to your bird that will help you understand what he exactly wants.

5. Managing bad behavior

One of the hardest things to do with your macaw is dealing with bad behavior. Since these birds are strong and powerful, issues like nipping or biting can get out of hand very easily. You can, however, manage any behavior quite easily if you are willing to be patient and calm.

This section gives you all the tips you need with respect to taking care of bad behavior in your bird.

These are the two primary causes for several behavioral issues in macaws.

It is very easy for them to figure out ways to manipulate their owners and thus develop behavioral issues. For example, if you pay attention to your bird when he screams, even if it means that you are asking him to stop, he will learn that this will shift your focus on him.

Boredom is the number one cause for all behavioral issues in birds including feather plucking. They also tend to mutilate their own skin in the process. It is mandatory for you to understand how you can keep your bird entertained enough that he does not develop these issues.

If the diet of the bird is not good enough and he lives on a poor diet for several years on end, behavioral problems can also develop due to poor nutrition. This is why vets recommend that you ensure that you have enough knowledge about birds before you bring one home.

The common behavioral issues with macaws are:

Chewing

While chewing is a natural behavior for birds, it can become a problem when chewing is directed at your valuable belongings. In the wild, a macaw will chew on branches and twigs to make his nest or home "customized".

Chewing is also very important for the bird to maintain his beak and keep it sharp. But, when it is not supervised and directed correctly, chewing can even become hazardous. For instance, a bird can chew on electric wires and get electrocuted or even start an electrical fire.

It is necessary for you to "parrot proof" your home to make it safe for the bird and also to keep your valuables out of the way. You can bring your bird several toys that they are allowed to chew on. This includes cuttlebones, branches, hard toys and lots more. Keep rotating these toys over the weeks to ensure that your bird remains interested in them.

Also make sure that your bird is always supervised when he is out of the cage. There is always a chance of accidents when you fail to do so.

Biting
The manner in which you approach your bird is very important. If you have any feelings of stress, anxiety or nervousness, your bird will catch on to it immediately. Any apprehension when you approach the bird leads to a defensive bite. Remember, birds don't think much, they react to the stimulus that they get.

Another common cause for biting is using your hands to punish the bird. If you shoo the bird with a sharp wave or perhaps toss things at the bird, a negative association is created immediately.

What you can do is help your bird associate the hand with positive things. Hand feeding or giving the bird treats with your hand tells them that they have nothing to worry about when you approach them.

Lastly, territorial behavior makes the bird nippy. This happens especially when they are nesting or in their breeding season. Females tend to be more hormonal and territorial.

There are some things that you can do when the bird bites in order to correct the behavior:

- When the bird is about to bite, blow on his face gently to distract him.

- If your bird is perched on your arm when he is about to bite, just drop your hand by a few inches. This will put the bird out of balance. And any bird hates an unsteady perch. He will immediately learn that biting makes him lose balance.

- Just put the bird down on the floor if he bites. They are not happy being on the ground as it makes them feel vulnerable and will immediately distract them.

The one thing that you should never do is scream or shout at the bird. This is a response to the bird's behavior and that is precisely what he is looking for.

Training your bird to step up and to make him associate your hands with positive things is a sure shot way of keeping your bird's biting behavior at bay.

Screaming

Vocalizing at a certain time of the day, particularly at dawn and dusk is common for blue macaws. The only time you have an issue is when the screaming is a result of your going away from your bird or the bird not getting his way.

The best way to prevent screaming in blue macaws is to make sure that you ignore the bird completely. That means you must not even look at the bird. Yelling at the bird and asking him to stop only reinforces the behavior.

Then, reward the bird when he behaves appropriately. For example, if the bird begins to scream when you leave the room, let him do so. The moment he stops screaming and you can count up to 5 or 10, reward him.

You can also look for specific triggers that are making your bird scream. If it is something that threatens the bird, for instance a large bright object, just get it out of his sight to calm him down.

Ignoring the screaming bird is a habit that everyone in your family must practice. You need to make sure that no one responds to the bird with any sound or eye contact.

Redirecting your bird with foraging toys before you leave the room is one way of calming him down when screaming is associated with separation anxiety.

Phobia or anxiety

The first thing that you need to understand is the difference between phobia and fear. Fear is a good thing as long as it is rational. This includes your bird being wary of new people, new toys or a new environment. This can be reversed by familiarizing the bird with the change.

On the other hand, phobia is the excessive and irrational need to get away from a particular situation, object or person. You know that your bird is phobic when he will do anything he can to get away from his object of terror. This includes:

- Running in place
- Pushing his head through the cage bars, sometimes till he bleeds
- Crashing into walls violently
- Resisting strongly
- Aggressive response such as biting
- Throwing himself on the back to appear dead
- Fear of coming out of the cage
- Self-mutilation
- Feather plucking.

You will mostly find phobias in birds that have been rescued from long term abuse and neglect. Improper breeding practices that do not allow the chick to develop properly can also lead to phobias. If the bird is force-weaned, the emotional development of the bird is stunted, leading to irrational fears.

There are several other factors such as a lack of socialization, being separated from other chicks in the flock too early, clipping the wings improperly or any traumatic injury or accident will lead to phobia in your bird.

That said, some birds are also genetically predisposed to being more anxious. You can seek your vet's assistance to provide medication to your bird to calm him down and reduce anxiety if you notice that it is affecting the well-being of your bird.

Interacting with your bird and trying to gain his trust will also go a long way in helping him overcome his phobia and become more confident.

Jealousy

Macaws can become jealous of new people in your family very easily. For instance, if you get married, the macaw may become jealous of your spouse. The real issue is when the jealousy is targeted towards a newborn.

Show the bird that having the person he is jealous of in the same room means that he has some advantages. This could be a gentle rub on the head or even a treat. Normally, when we have a newborn in the house, especially, we tend to ignore the bird in the presence of the baby. So, the bird quickly associates the child with neglect. You do not have to let the bird out of the cage, of course. With the baby or any other person that the jealously is targeted at in the same room, have some interaction with your bird.

Encourage the other person to build a relationship with the bird. This can mean giving the bird a treat occasionally and eventually encouraging the bird to step up on the person's hand or finger. The more the bird trusts the other person, the less he will be jealous.

This is not something you can accomplish in a day or even a few days. It will take time for your bird to trust another person completely.

All you need to be aware of is the information that you are passing on to the bird. If you are away from your bird every time that person is around, jealousy will build. Instead, both of you can try and interact with the bird and shower him with the attention he wants.

Feather plucking
If your bird suddenly begins to pluck his own feathers out in an agitated manner or over-preens himself to the extent that he mutilates his skin and feathers, then it means that he has developed the issue of feather plucking.

When your bird resorts to feather plucking, you will see several bald spots. In addition to that, you will find feathers on the floor of the cage even when it is not molting season.

There are several reasons for feather plucking in blue macaws including;
- **Malnutrition:** If the diet of the bird is deprived of minerals like zinc, calcium, selenium and manganese, the skin becomes irritable leading to feather plucking.

- **Boredom:** When the cage is too small for the bird to move around or if he does not have enough activities to keep him mentally stimulated, feather plucking becomes a means to keep himself engaged.

- **Lack of natural light:** Sunlight is a source of vitamin D. If your bird is kept in a dark area for long hours, he will become very depressed. This manifests in the form of feather plucking.

- **Stress:** If your bird is unwell or if he is in an environment that makes him feel stressed, such as a pet lurking around the cage very often, then feather plucking will begin. There are some medicines and supplements that can help him overcome feather plucking associated with stress. Treating the primary health issue will also reduce feather plucking in your bird.

- **Loneliness:** Blue macaws are solitary birds in the wild. However, it does not mean that they do not need any companionship. Spending time with your bird or finding him a compatible cage mate can help solve feather plucking related to loneliness.

- **Pain:** With birds, pain is not a feeling that they are able to understand. They know that they are uncomfortable and will try to relieve themselves by plucking feathers off the area where the pain is concentrated. There are also health issues like Psittacosis and Aspergillosis that have been commonly associated with feather plucking in birds. Your bird may have ingested a foreign object that makes his crop irritable, leading to this behavioral issue.

- **Food allergies:** Sensitivity towards a certain type of food will lead to feather plucking. Changing the diet or the brand of food that you give your bird is an effective way to deal with feather plucking.

In addition to the above, hormonal imbalance, improper diet and toxicosis can also lead to feather plucking in birds. Since there are so many causes for this condition, it is best that you let your vet examine the bird first before you begin to treat your bird.

Once the primary causal factor is eliminated, there are several medicines that will help the feathers grow back. You can also spray the body with an aloe vera solution to make the skin less irritable and promote the growth of feathers.

Chapter 5: Breeding your Blue Macaw

With blue macaws, you need to be very sure that you want to breed the bird and have the facilities to do so before you start a program in your home.

These birds are extremely expensive and a lot of things could go wrong. Here are a few considerations that must make before you bring a blue macaw home:

- They are very expensive birds. If you end up with an incompatible pair, you may have several issues raising your bird and maintaining them.

- The breeding program may not always be successful. Birds like the Spix Macaw do not breed easily in captivity. There are highly specialized programs that work on breeding these birds to simple save their population.

- Once you have your baby macaws, what do you want to do with them? If you want to sell them, do you have any buyers? If you want to keep them, do you have the necessary resources?

1. How to find a mate

If you have a single blue macaw parrot at home, introducing a mate can be tricky. When they are hormonal, females especially, tend to be territorial and aggressive. She is the one that sets the tone of the courting period. If the birds are left unsupervised, the female can cause severe injuries and can potentially kill the male bird.

You will know that a female blue macaw is ready to mate when you see her spending a lot of time in the nesting box. You must never introduce a male companion immediately. Start by placing the cage of the male bird near the female's cage and allow them to get used to one another.

When the female is adjusted to the presence of her potential mate, she will show signs of being interested in him. To begin with, she will be seen clinging on to the cage bar on the side that is close to the cage of the male bird.

The male will respond with pinning of his eyes and the female will keep her head tilted backwards. Even when they are in this stage, it is advisable to keep them apart. You can do this for about one more week till you are certain that the female is interested in the male bird.

Once she shows genuine interest, you can place the birds together. It is best to put them in a different cage altogether. If not, you must put the female bird in the cage of the male and not vice versa.

This will prevent excessive territorial behavior from the female. Nevertheless, you can expect the female to chase the male bird around in the cage. That is when you need to be extra attentive. If you notice any signs of aggression, it means that you will have to separate them and try again or will have to look for a new mate altogether.

During the introduction, clipping the wings of the female bird is a good idea while keeping the wings of the male intact. That way, the female will have enough flight to reach up to the nesting box. As for the male bird, he will be able to escape any sudden attack.

If you want to pair two birds in particular but are finding it hard to get them to be compatible, you can try by changing the location of the cage or putting them in a new age. When they are introduced in a completely unfamiliar environment, they tend to bond with one another and will also become less aggressive.

Make sure that new interactions are supervised for a few weeks to let the birds become comfortable with one another.

The other option is to house a pair together all year around. This is a better option as the aggressive behavior is curbed. Since the female has bonded with the male over the year, the chances of her trying to attack him will be highly reduced.

They become more affectionate towards one another and will do everything together throughout the year. Then when the breeding season arrives, they will show more interest in one another.

After this, you can be sure that they will mate and lay their first clutch. Keeping a pair together for a year is a lot more beneficial. You will be able to maintain proper records. You will also be able to predict the types of mutations that may occur with the birds you pair.

2. Creating the right breeding conditions

Birds require very specific conditions in order to breed. They are shy creatures and will not breed if there is too much disturbance. You need to first shift the cage of the birds to a room in the house that is quiet, but has a good supply of natural light. You can lay a cloth over the cage for the birds to escape into when they want to rest.

Unless there is a proper nesting place available for the birds, they are very unlikely to mate. Keeping a nesting box just outside the cage will encourage them to mate. The cage should be fixed at a height from the floor of the cage. It can be placed on the play area of you have a play top cage.

Instead of using cardboard boxes, it best to get a store made nesting box for your blue macaw. These nesting boxes made of wood or metal are not destroyed easily. They can be used for all the breeding seasons making the birds feel comfortable. These boxes are also easier to clean. You need to remember that blue macaw chicks can be very messy.

Choose a vertical nesting box that measures at least 18X18X36 inches. These boxes usually have an entrance door and a separate inspection door that you can access.

The nesting box should be placed in such a way that the birds have a good view of the room around them. The cage should have solid perch for the birds. Place one inside the cage and one outside leading to the nest box. This allows them to access the nest. These perches should be made of hardwood as the females are likely to chew on them when they become hormonal.

Leaving a few soft wood options is a good idea to help the bird chew it and release some stress. With this arrangement, your birds will get ready to mate. The male will mount the female a couple of times. In two weeks the female will lay her first clutch of eggs that consists of 2-4 eggs that are white in color.

The incubation period is about 22 days during which the hen will care for the eggs on her own.

Feeding the female

You need to make sure that the birds have adequate nutrients to produce the necessary hormones and have a successful breeding season. For the females, especially, the diet is of utmost importance.

Adding assorted nuts to the diet will help the bird to a large extent. Each nut has specific functions that aid the breeding season. Here are a few nuts that you should include and the benefits of these nuts:

- Macadamia nuts- They provide the additional fats that are required in a bird's diet during this season.
- Walnuts- They provide the birds with necessary omega 3 fatty acids.
- Filberts- They are a great source of calcium for the females.
- Pistachios- They add vitamin A in large amounts.

In addition to that you can also provide coconut, eggs and fresh fruits and vegetables. The nutrition of the bird determines the final quality of the eggs that are produced during this season.

You can even provide fortified pellets or supplements under the guidance of your vet to give your birds the additional nutrition boost that they require.

3. Artificially hatching the eggs

Macaws usually abandon their clutch after a few days. This is when you need to intervene and take care of the eggs yourself. Sometimes you will also notice that the hen also destroys a couple of the eggs.

To incubate the eggs, you can purchase a standard incubator from any pet supplies store. You can also order them online. It is never advisable to prepare your own incubator as the temperature settings need to be very accurate to hatch the eggs successfully. The incubation period will be the same as the natural incubation period.

The incubator is a one-time investment that is completely worth it if you choose to breed more blue macaws even in the next season.

Here are a few tips to incubate the eggs correctly:

- Pick the eggs up with clean hands. The chicks are extremely vulnerable to diseases and can be affected even with the smallest traces of microbes. Only pick eggs that are visibly clean. If there is a lot of debris or poop on a certain egg, it is best not to mix it with the other eggs as it will cause unwanted infections.

- Wash the eggs gently to clean the surface. The next step is to candle the eggs. This means you will have to hold the egg up to a light. If you can see the embryo in the form of a dark patch, it means that the egg is fertile. On the other hand, if all you can see is an empty space inside the egg, it is probably not going to hatch.

- In the natural setting, the eggs are usually given heat on one side while the other side remains cooler. Then the hen may turn the eggs with her movements. It is impossible to heat the egg evenly even if you have a fan type incubator that heats up the interior of the egg quite evenly.

- The next thing to keep in mind is the transfer from the nest box to the incubator. Line a container with wood shavings and place the eggs away from each other. Even the slightest bump can crack an egg. You need to know that a cracked egg has very few chances of hatching.

- The incubator will also have a humidifier that will maintain the moisture levels inside the incubator. The temperature and the humidity should be set as per the readings advised for macaws. That is the ideal condition for the eggs to hatch.

- In case you want to be doubly sure, you can also check the temperature with a mercury thermometer regularly.

- It is safest to place the eggs on the side when you put them in the incubator. They are stable and will not have any damage or accidents.

- Heating the eggs evenly is the most important thing when it comes to the chances of hatching the egg. Make sure you turn the eggs every two hours over 16 hours. This should be done an odd number of times. The next step is to turn the eggs by 180 degrees once every day.

- Keep a close watch on the eggs in the incubator. It is best that you get an incubator with a see through lid. This will let you observe and monitor the eggs. If you notice that one of them has cracked way before the incubation period ends, take it out of the incubator. If the eggs have a foul smelling discharge, begin to take an abnormal shape or change color, you need to remove them as they could be carrying diseases that will destroy the whole clutch.

- Usually, blue macaw eggs will pip after 24-48 hours of the completion of the incubation period.

- The hatching of the egg begins when the carbon dioxide levels in the egg increase. This starts the hatching process. All baby birds have an egg tooth which allows them to tear the inner membrane open. Then they continue to tear the egg shell to come out.

- The muscles of the chick twitch in order to strengthen them and to make sure that he is able to tear the egg shell out successfully.

- Never try to assist the hatching process unless you are a professional. If you feel like your chicks are unable to break out of the egg shell, you can call your vet immediately.

Watching the eggs hatch is a magical experience. You can do a few small things to make your clutch more successful. For instance, if you are buying a brand new incubator, turn on the recommended settings and keep it on for at least two weeks before you expect the eggs to be placed in them.

Make sure that the incubator is not disturbed. Keep all the wires tucked in to prevent someone from tripping on it and disturbing the set up or turning the incubator off. It is best to place this incubator in areas like the basement that are seldom used by you or your family members.

4. Raising the chicks

Hand raised chicks are certainly tamer. But, if you do not really need a very tame chick, co-parenting with your blue macaw is a good idea. You can provide one meal while the parents provide the others. You can work your way up by increasing the number of feeds you give the baby birds.

You may have to hand raise the baby entirely if the eggs have been hatched in an incubator or if the mother abandons the nest. This will require some commitment and a lot of patience.

You will have to feed the baby birds every two hours, even at night. So, you need to be entirely sure that you can continue to do so before you take up this responsibility.

In case you are unable to hand feed the bird or if you think that it is too much work, you can contact your avian vet. There are also several breeders who will be able to foster the chicks.

Ideally, the mother bird should provide for her babies. This will allow the mother to transfer certain nutrients into the baby's body that will help develop a strong immune system.

What you need to know about hand feeding

- It is a tedious task. Newborn chicks are difficult to handle as they will move around a lot and will get away from you in a jiffy.

- The delicate frame of the bird's body can also be very intimidating to handle.

- Make sure your hands are properly disinfected before you can handle the baby bird.

- If the eggs have been hatched in an incubator, do not feed the bird for up to 6 hours after hatching. If you feed the baby too early, it could be fatal.

- If you are co-parenting the bird, you must first place it in a brooder with an internal temperature of 95 degree Fahrenheit. When the baby is warmed up, you can feed him. If you feel like he is panting or showing discomfort, reduce the temperature.

- When the baby is warm enough, you can feed him. In case the crop is already full with the food provided by the parent birds, wait for it to empty. If food is present in the crop, a milky fluid is seen in the area.

- A syringe or an eye dropper is ideal to feed the baby birds.

Handfeeding tips for one day old blue macaw chicks:
- The food must be warm and should be about 105-108 degrees Fahrenheit in temperature.

- If it is the first feed of the bird, using only an electrolyte solution is recommended.

- The feeding utensils should be cleaned thoroughly.

- The baby should be kept warm at all times. If the body becomes too cool, the digestion process is hampered.

- The bedding in the brooder should be changed every time you feed your baby bird.

- If there is any abnormality, contact your avian vet immediately.

- If your chick is refusing to eat, do not force him.

- The crop should never be over filled as it can lead to issues like sour crop.

- A couple of drops should be good enough during the bird's first few feeds.

- The bird should be fed every two hours or just before the crop is fully empty.

The first feed

The bird must be handled very gently to make sure that you do not startle or injure the baby bird. Here are a few important guidelines to make the first feeding session less stressful.

- It is recommended that you use some electrolyte solution such as pedialyte that is not flavored.

- The purpose of the electrolyte solution is to make sure that the digestive abilities of the bird are fine.

- When he has emptied the crop, he is ready for the commercially prepared bird formula.

- To give the bird electrolyte, place a small drop on the left side of the bird's mouth. In most cases, the baby will lap it up immediately.

- In case the baby does not show any interest in the food, you have the option of letting him rest for some time and then trying again.

- Some baby chicks will have to practice before they are able to understand how to take in handfed food.

- If after several attempts, your baby bird is not taking any food in, it is possible that the food is not warm enough.

- Dipping the syringe or ink dropper in a glass of warm water before feeding the bird is the best way to keep it warm enough.

5. Weaning

You can wean a baby bird when he is about 4 weeks old. Weaning means to make the bird capable of eating his food without any assistance.

This will take some understanding and training for your baby bird. So you need to be as patient as possible.

Begin by leaving cubes of fresh fruit on the floor of the cage and let the bird inspect it. Since blue macaws are curious by nature, they will peck at it and try to understand the new food.

They may just leave the food alone and walk away or may try to take a piece off. Let the bird explore and after one hour of providing fresh fruits and vegetables, the cage should be cleaned out to prevent chances of spoiling foods lying around the cage.

As the bird gets familiar with the new food, he will eat bits of it. Take a note of the types of fruits and vegetables that your bird seems to like and include them in the diet.

Soon, you will see that the bird will begin to lose interest in the formula as he will be full with the food that he has eaten by himself. You can even try to leave pellets and seeds in the water bowl. As the quantity of eating foods on their own increases, the need for assistance will decrease. That way you will have a bird who has been weaned correctly.

Chapter 6: Health Concerns with Blue Macaws

Like all parrot species, blue macaws are also prone to health issues. These issues can become serious if you do not notice the initial symptoms. With macaws, you need to pay attention to the slightest deviation from normal behavior. Since these birds tend to hide symptoms, the disease usually is at a very serious stage before you actually notice it.

As a prey animal, birds do not reveal symptoms as it makes them vulnerable in the wild. The best thing that you can do is take preventive measures by providing the right nutrition and sanitary conditions for the bird to thrive in.

The top priority for a bird owner is to find a good vet who can provide you with necessary information and suggestions to take good care of your bird.

1. Finding a vet for your Blue Macaw

This is the most crucial part in providing good care for your bird. With birds, you will require someone who specializes in treating health issues specific to them. While your local vet can be very helpful in treating emergencies, you will require a specialized avian vet to help you maintain the health of your blue macaw.

An avian vet has dedicated his practice to treating exotic birds and understanding their anatomy. While their educational qualification is the same as a vet who works with pets like dogs or cat, his practice involve birds.

Avian vets are often part of authorized organizations like the Association of Avian Vets. This helps them stay updated and learn about the new techniques of treating health issues related to birds.

If you are a new parrot owner, your avian vet will be a reliable source of information for you.

Locating your avian vet

The most difficult part about having a pet bird is locating a qualified avian vet. There are a few resources that you can try to find good leads:

- The yellow pages is the best way to start. This will have a list of specialized vets along with their qualifications.

- The official website of the Association of Avian vets will list a number of qualified avian vets who will be able to care for your bird.

- You can contact the veterinary medical association in your state for information.

- Speak to other bird owners and look for reliable vets in your vicinity.

The closer your vet is to your home the easier it will be to take your bird for a checkup. Additionally, a vet who is located nearby will be able to deal with emergencies more effectively.

What to ask the vet

To be sure that you have chosen the right vet to treat your bird, here are a few questions that you should ask him or her upon your first visit:

- **How long have they been working with birds?** The more experience they have, the better qualified they are. You need to find someone who has a solid background to make sure that your beloved pet is in good hands.

- **Have you worked with blue macaws before?** Although it may seem like all parrots are the same, each species has its own requirement and demands. The more your vet has worked with the species of parrot that you have, the more experience they will have.

- **Are you part of the AAV?** While it doesn't mean that a vet who is not part of this organization is not qualified enough, someone who is part of it is definitely a lot more reassuring. You see the AAV only promotes highest quality medical healthcare for birds and ensures that all its members are updated.

- **Do you have birds at home?** It is certainly an advantage if your vet is a bird owner. That will give him a lot of hands on experience with the body language of the bird which will help make treatment sessions less stressful.

- **Is there an after-hours facility or emergency facility?** An accident does not occur with warning. So you need a vet who can be available or make some medical assistance available to your bird should some such incident occur.

- **What are your fees?** This is definitely a question you should ask, even if you feel awkward about it. If you are unable to afford the veterinary charges of a certain vet, you can look for more options. Every vet will have a fee schedule chart that will tell you what exactly you can expect when you sign up for a service.

- **Are house calls an option?** In some cases, the bird may be too severely injured or unwell to take him to the vet. Then, it will become necessary for the vet to come to you.

- **How many examinations are recommended per year?** Usually, a vet will recommend about one thorough examination per year. This is done to make sure that your bird is always in good health.

A qualified avian vet will answer all your questions patiently and without any hesitation. The manner in which they respond to questions will also tell you if their personality is compatible to you or not. This goes a long way in building a good relationship with your vet.

Other considerations
- Watch how your vet interacts with the bird on the first visit. They must be confident to handle the bird and should be comfortable.

- How does the staff help to make the visit less stressful for the bird? Are they interacting with you in a good manner?

Once you are convinced that a certain vet is perfect for your bird, you will be in partnership with them to provide a healthy life for your bird.

2. Identifying illnesses in birds
With macaws, the biggest issue is identifying illnesses at an early stage to make sure that the bird gets the care that he needs. Now, like any other parrot, they are great at concealing the symptoms, allowing the disease to

become more intense. However, there are some very subtle signs that you will have to watch out for.

The more you interact with your bird, the more familiar you will become with these signs. That way, you can get them medical attention immediately and avert an unfavorable situation.

Hiding an illness is a part of the bird's instinct to survive. If a predator is able to identify a sick bird, he will become an easy prey. That is why birds pretend to be absolutely in good health for as long as they can.

The most common signs of illness in blue macaws are:

- **The feathers:** A bird who is healthy will look alter, will have bright eyes and will look perfectly preened. The feathers are held close to the body. On the other hand, a bird who is unwell will keep his feathers puffed up and ruffled for long hours.

  The feathers will also be maintained poorly as the bird is too unwell to preen. The feathers will appear tattered, dirty and matted. The feather in the vent area should be especially clean. If you see that there is feces stuck on these feathers, it indicates some digestive issue.

- **Posture:** When the bird is perched, he should be upright with the weight distributed evenly on the feet. The tip of the wing should cross over at the back and the tail feathers should remain straight.

  If you notice drooping wings with the tail drawn inwards, it shows some discomfort. In addition to this, any low posture or wobbly stance on the perch is an indication of abnormality. Any indication of constant weight shift and restlessness is a sign of injury or any dysfunction in the feet because of a disease. In some cases, this can be an indication of tumors in the kidney.

- **Attitude:** The bird will show behavioral changes when he is sick. You will notice that the level of activity decreases. The bird will also vocalize a lot less when he is unwell. There may be drastic changes in the personality. For instance, a friendly bird might suddenly become irritable and aggressive or a bird who is normally aggressive is suddenly very easy to handle. Either way, you have some abnormality in the bird.

- **The beak:** In birds, the beak is growing constantly. This is because normal activity leads to some wear and tear that needs to be repaired. If you notice that the beak is growing too fast or if you see that the quality of the beak is deteriorating, then the bird may have developed health issues.

  For instance, when the bird has any liver disease, you will notice black spots on the beak with an overgrowth. So, abnormal rate of growth should not be taken lightly. Look for any crust on enlargement in the mouth and the beak of the bird.

- **The feet:** No matter how many precautions you take, birds tend to develop infections in the feet. There are pressure sores that develop when the perch is improper. Some of the most common issues that you will see in the feet are soreness in the feet, lameness, swelling, redness and constant weight shift.

  If any of these problems are associated with the leg band, make sure it is removed immediately. If there is any flakiness or crustiness on the feet, it is a sign of a parasitic infection or any nutritional deficiency.

- **The respiratory tract:** In healthy birds, breathing is very comfortable and does not require any effort. If the bird continues to breathe hard even when he is at rest, it is an indication of some issue. There must not be any noises when the bird is breathing. Sounds like wheezing, clicking or sneezing are an indication of illness in the bird.

  You will also notice nasal discharge in the bird with some staining on the feathers covering the area just above the nostril. Pink eye or conjunctivitis is also common when there are respiratory issues. This leads to redness and swelling along with some discharge near the eyes.

  A bird who is finding it hard to breathe is easy to recognize. The mouth will remain open and the bird will actually gasp for breath. Besides infections in the respiratory tract, labored breathing is also the result of abdominal infections.

You will see the bird bob his tail up and down, showing that there is some enlargement in the abdomen or some form of respiratory tract infection. Heart disease can also be indicated by labored breathing.

- **Consumption of food:** The bird will be unable to eat well when he is sick. With the rate of metabolism that is prevalent in their bodies, this can be a serious issue.

You need to keep an eye on the food consumed by your bird on a daily basis. The seeds when eaten are hulled and then swallowed. On the other hand, the bird will just pick up the seed and drop it on the floor when he is not interested.

At times, the bird may eat the seed without hulling, leaving hulled seeds on the floor of the cage. This can also be caused when the bird is vomiting or regurgitating.

Regurgitation is common in blue macaws as it is a type of courtship behavior. If the bird has been vomiting, you will see that the ejected food will stick to the floor and the bars of the cage.

- **Consumption of water:** Although it may seem like the bird does not drink too much water, it is necessary to make sure that he gets enough clean water to drink. Whether the bird drinks too much water or very little water, it is a sign of some metabolic issue or an issue related to the digestive tract of the bird. Just keep a tab on how much water is left in the bowl when you clean it out everyday. If it is more or less than usual, contact your vet to be entirely sure.

- **Droppings:** One of the best indicators of health is the dropping of the bird. If you see that the frequency reduces or increases, keep an eye on the bird. If reduced food intake is the reason for reduced droppings, talk to your vet.

It is true that the droppings will change color when different foods are consumed. However, if you notice abnormal coloration, it can indicate health problems in the bird. If the consistency of the dropping changes, it can also be an indication of digestive issues or other health disorders. Cleaning the bedding and substrate regularly will help you keep an eye on the droppings.

Any signs of blood in the droppings is certainly a red flag. There are several issues related to the cloaca, the oviduct and the digestive tract that leads to this. It can also be a warning sign for a tumor that is developing on the body of the bird.

- **Unusual growth on the body:** Cysts on the feathers, abscesses or any swelling on the body must be reported to the vet. The bird must not have any fat deposit on the abdomen and the chest. If you see any enlargement in the body, it could be a sign of a tumor. Handling your bird regularly and keeping an eye on these issues will help you seek help at early stages of the disease. The more you interact with your bird, the easier it is to detect any growth or abnormality on his body.

Now that you have a fair idea about how different symptoms manifest, the only thing that you need to do is keep an eye on your bird. Inspect the cage regularly and also handle your bird as frequently as you can.

Annual examinations that include a fecal analysis and blood tests are highly recommended. They can help you detect any abnormality at the earliest. That way the chances of recovery from any illness is also high.

If you do have a few false alarms once in a while, it does not mean that you are overprotective. The more cautious you are, the healthier your bird will be.

3. Common health issues

There are a few infections and diseases that you need to know about as they commonly affect the blue macaw as a species. We will talk about the identification, the cause and the cure for these conditions in the following section:

Proventricular Dilation Disease

This condition is also known as Macaw Wasting Syndrome. In the past, this condition was considered to be fatal most of the time. However, new treatment methods have emerged over the years, which makes it possible to control the symptoms in the early stages.

This condition is caused by the Avian Bornavirus which is believed to have spread rampantly due to pet trade across the world. These viruses invade the cell of the host and continue to infect more cells eventually. The incubation period for this virus is about 4 weeks. It affects younger birds usually, although a blue macaw is vulnerable at any age, especially during the breeding season. It can be spread from the hen to the eggs as well.

The common signs of PDD are:

- Poor digestion
- Traces of undigested foods in the feces.
- Sudden increase or decrease in appetite
- Weight loss
- Depression
- Anorexia
- Lack of coordination
- Seizures
- Muscle deficiencies
- Feather plucking
- Constant crying or moaning

The treatment of this condition includes administration of anti-inflammatory drugs that can soothe the symptoms. However, the infection itself is seldom cured. Supplements like milk thistle and elemental formula for avians are also recommended.

Psittacine Beak and Feather Disease

With this condition, the cells of the feather and beak are killed by a strain of virus called the circovirus. This disease also impairs the immune system of the bird, leading to death of the bird from other infections in most cases.

This condition was first noticed among cockatoos but has affected several species of birds, mostly those belonging to the Psittacine family.

In most cases, death follows the infection. However, if the bird responds positively to the tests but has no signs of the diseases physically, it means that he or she is a carrier of the condition. This is when you have to quarantine the bird immediately. This is a contagious disease that spreads very easily.

The common signs of PBFD are:

- Abnormalities in the feathers
- Bumps and uneven edges in the beak
- Missing lumps of feathers
- Loss of appetite
- Diarrhea
- Regurgitation

In most cases, the birds will die before they show the above symptoms.

Treatment of the condition includes administering probiotics and mineral or vitamin supplementation. The only way to curb PBFD is to take preventive measures such as maintaining good sanitation and diet.

Psittacosis

This condition is also known as Chlamydiosis or Parrot fever. The threat with this condition is that it can also affect human beings. It is a condition caused by a certain strain of bacteria called the Chlamydia Psittaci.

A few species of birds may never show symptoms of this condition and could be mere carriers. However, the fact that humans are susceptible to the condition requires you to take additional precautions.

This bacterial infection is only spread when you come in contact with the feces of the bird. This is true for other birds as well. So, maintaining good hygiene is the first step towards preventing this condition among the other birds in your aviary. You must also make sure that your birds are not exposed to the feces of wild birds when you let them out. The common problems leading to chlamydiosis are overcrowding of the aviary, improper quarantine measures etc.

The common signs of Chlamydiosis or Psittacosis are:
- Labored breathing
- Infection of the sinuses
- Runny nasal passage

- Discharge and swelling of the eyes
- Ruffled feathers
- Lethargy
- Dehydration
- Weight loss
- Abnormal droppings

These are the mild symptoms of the condition. In case of a chronic case of Psittacosis you will observe unusual positioning of the head, tremors, lack of co-ordination, paralysis of the legs and loss of control over the muscles.

The birds suspected with this condition are tested for a high WBC count and an increase in liver enzymes, which suggests liver damage. Antibiotics like Doxycycline and Tetracycline are usually administered to affected birds. In addition to that supplements and medicated foods are also provided. However, because most birds refuse to eat when affected with this condition, it becomes a lot harder to give them proper treatment.

Aspergillosis
This is a condition that is non contagious but highly infectious. The fungus that causes this condition is known as Aspergillus Fumigatus and is known to be very opportunistic. That is why, even the slightest signs of dampness will become breeding grounds for this fungi.

Young birds are mostly susceptible to this condition. In case of juvenile or baby birds, the rate of mortality is extremely high. Of course, in case of adult birds, they could become infected too. The spores of this fungus are easily inhaled as they are extremely small. That is why the infection is mostly seen in the air capillaries of the affected bird.

The most common signs of aspergillosis include:

- Polydipsia or abnormal thirst
- Stunted growth
- Lethargy
- Ruffled feathers
- Anorexia
- Polyuria or large amounts of urine in the excreta
- Wheezing

- Coughing
- Nasal Discharge
- Tremors
- Ataxia or loss of control over the limbs
- Cloudy eyes

This condition mainly affects the respiratory tract. However, other organs may also be affected in some rare cases of infection. Treatment of this condition is challenging because of the loss of immunity in birds. So the affected bird could also have multiple infections caused by other microorganisms. Normally, systemic antifungal therapy is recommended. The lesions caused at the site of infection may also be removed through suction or surgery.

Preventive care is the best way to keep your bird safe. Maintaining a high standard of husbandry will help you control infections by depriving the fungus of any breeding sites.

Avian sinusitis
It is quite common for the sinuses of the birds to get infected. This condition is mostly associated with a deficiency in Vitamin A. This leads to abnormal cell division that will be seen in the form of thickened mucus around the eyes. This can further lead to abscesses or conjunctivitis in the affected bird. There are debates about the causal factor, however.

The earliest signs of this condition are:
- Clicking
- Proptosis or protrusion of the eyeball
- Sneezing
- Excessive secretion of mucus

Later on, you will notice that there is swelling around the eyes as well as the region around the beak of the bird. When the sinus is infected, it is also possible for the bird to be suffering from associated conditions such as pneumonia.

A needle biopsy of the area with swelling helps diagnose the condition. This helps you differentiate the condition form abscesses that require a completely different treatment altogether.

The bird is treated with an antibiotic called Baytril that can curb any infection by bacteria such as pseudomonas. In addition to this, the bird also requires Vitamin A supplementation which may be administered through an intramuscular injection. The sinus is flushed if the swelling is too much.

You must also improve the diet of the bird and include as many dark green vegetables as possible. Oranges are also recommended to improve the condition. Lastly, you need to include only fortified pellets in your bird's diet to help restore the Vitamin A levels in the body.

Psittacine Herpes Virus
Also known as Pacheco's disease, this condition was first recognized in the country of Brazil. Aviculturists observed that birds began to die within few days of being unwell. In less than 3-4 days, a herpes virus infection will cause nasal discharge and abnormal feces. This condition is very contagious and is often fatal.

New World parrots like the four blue macaws are more susceptible to this condition. This condition is generally transmitted through the feces or the nasal discharge. The problem with this virus is that it remains stable even outside the body of the host.

It will be seen on different surfaces in the cage, the food and the water bowls. As a result, it spreads quite easily. Of course, there are possibilities of transmission of this condition from the mother to the embryo.

In many cases, a bird could be a mere carrier of the condition without any symptoms. A bird that has survived an infection is a potential threat to you flock.

The symptoms of this condition commonly include:
- Ruffled Feathers
- Diarrhea
- Sinusitis
- Anorexia
- Conjunctivitis
- Tremors in the neck, legs and wings
- Lethargy

- Weight loss
- Green colored Feces

In most cases, death occurs due to enlargement in the liver or the spleen. When subjected to stress and sudden climate changes, the virus can get activated in birds that are carrier, leading to their death.

A PCR test is conducted to screen the birds for a herpes virus infection. In some cases a bird that is tested positive could show no symptoms at all.

There is no known cure for this condition. Only preventive measures can be taken by keeping the cage conditions pristine. You also need to ensure that your bird does not undergo any stress or trauma. When he is not well exercised or mentally stimulated, there are chances of activation of this strain of virus.

Coacal papillomas

This is yet another condition that is said to be caused by a strain of virus called Papillomavirus. This condition leads to benign tumors in the regions of the bird's body that are unfeathered. There are a few debates about the causal factors of this condition, however. This is because of the internal lesions detected with this condition that is caused by a strain of Herpes virus.

Common symptoms of the condition include:
• Wart like growths on the legs and feet
• Loose droppings
• Dried fecal matter around the vent area
• Blood in the droppings of the bird

In case you suspect this condition in your macaw, you can make a preemptive diagnosis at home. Apply a small amount of 5% acetic acid on the cloacal region. If this turns white, then your bird is mostly infected.

Proper diagnosis includes a biopsy of the tissue that is affected. The growth on the legs and feet will be removed surgically as the first step to treatment. This condition leads to a compromised immune system that can further lead to secondary infections by bacteria and other microorganisms.

If your bird harbors any internal papillomas, you need to have them monitored frequently for any infection in the GI tract. If left ignored, it can lead to tumors in the bile duct or the pancreas.

Kidney dysfunction

There are two kinds of kidney dysfunction that you will observe in bird:

Chronic renal failure: This is when the kidney becomes progressively dysfunctional. At the onset, the bird will show very few signs and will only seem mildly under the weather.
Acute renal failure: This is when both the kidneys fail and deteriorate rapidly. The condition is usually reversible but the kidneys will be compromised to a great extent.

So, how can you tell if your bird has developed any of these kidney diseases:
-   Polydipsia or excessive water consumption followed by frequent urination is common. This is the bird's attempt to flush out toxins from the blood as the kidney is unable to perform this function effectively.
-   Watery droppings
-   Enlargement of the abdomen
-   Constipation
-   Vomiting
-   Inability to fly
-   Fluffing of feathers
-   Depression
-   Lethargy
-   Weakness
-   Blood in the droppings
-   Dehydration
-   Swollen joints
-   Inability to walk or balance himself

These renal diseases can be caused by microbial infections. The common virus responsible for this condition is the Polyomavirus while the most common fungus seen is the Aspergillus fungi.

There are various other causes like excessive vitamin D consumption, allergy to any antibiotics or medication that has been administered, heavy metal poisoning, toxicity by pesticides and ingestion of certain plants.

Gout, which is the inability of the bird to release waste from the body, also leads to kidney failure over time.

Proper diagnosis of this condition requires a full medical history of the bird. This is followed by a physical examination, blood chemistry tests, blood count tests and a urine analysis. In ambiguous cases, cloacal swabs, endoscopy and ultrasound are used to confirm the condition that the bird has been affected with.

Supportive care, including tube feeding and providing the right supplements, aids recovery of the bird. It is recommended that the blood of the bird be tested on a regular basis to change the treatment method as required by the body of the bird.

Antibiotics may be administered as bacteria is the common cause of renal failure in birds. There could also be some secondary infections that need to be treated with an antibiotics. Besides this, depending upon the nature of the infection, antifungal and antiviral medicines are provided.

In the case of toxicity or gout, vitamin A supplementation is encouraged. There could also be surgical intervention if tumors or lesions are detected internally.

It is recommended that you include proteins, vitamin B complex, Vitamin C and Vitamin A in the diet of the bird. Foods like dandelion root, Cranberry, Parsley and Nettle tea will help improve the functioning of the kidneys and will aid in quick recovery of the affected bird.

Lipomas or Tumors

It is possible for pet birds to develop tumors or lipomas on their bodies. These are usually seen as bumps or lumps on the skin or just under the skin. Of course, every lump is not an indication of tumor as some of them could also be abscesses.

In many cases, what is feared to be a tumor could be a cyst that is covered with fluids or pus. These are not cancerous and will not spread like the tumors.

A tumor is a solid tissue mass that can grow very quickly and spread across the body of the bird. It can occur in any part of the body and needs immediate attention to ensure that your bird is able to recover from it.

There are two kinds of tumors: Benign and malignant. The benign tumors do not cause cancer while the malignant ones are cancerous. While both can adversely affect the health of the bird, benign tumors are less urgent that the malignant ones.

The reason for this is that the benign tumors do not spread to other parts of the bird's body like the malignant ones. There are chances of growth in this tumor but they almost never spread. Even if they do, there is enough time to provide medical care effectively.

That does not mean that you can ignore these tumors. They need to be removed at the earliest. Since they get bigger in size, they can put a lot of pressure on the internal organs of the bird leading to severe discomfort and even damage.

Malignant tumors will damage the nearby tissues of the affected organ as well. A process called metastasis is responsible for this. This is when the cell breaks away from the tumor and travels through the blood stream. Then it spreads to various parts of the body to cause multiple tumors.

Usually a tumor is caused by mutations in the DNA of the bird's cells. Normal cells will not divide uncontrollably like the tumors. They multiply enough to grow and repair the body.

There are several other factors like the environment of the bird, inclusion of carcinogens in the diet of the bird, nutritional deficiencies, old age and interbreeding that compromises the immune system of the bird, leading to this condition.

There are various types of tumors that can affect a bird. The most common one is that of the skin or the squamous cells of the skin. This leads to tumors near the eyes, around the preen gland, on the skin on the head and around the beak. A huge causal factor for this is self-mutilation by the birds. This is an external tumor that you can identify as lumps on the surface of the skin.

Another type of tumor that affects birds is a fibroid tumor. This affects the connective tissues of the bird. Usually, these tumors are benign. When they become malignant, the condition is known as fibrosarcoma. These tumors are also external and will be seen on the legs, wings, the beak and the sternum of the bird.

The most common type of internal tumor is a tumor in the reproductive organs or the kidneys. Again, these tumors could either be malignant or benign. The problem with these internal tumors is that they will go unnoticed until the bird falls severely sick. The pressure of these tumors on the internal organs leads to a lot of discomfort and stress for the birds. In most cases, the digestive system experiences a lot of stress, leading to improper digestion of food. The droppings are not excreted effectively from the body either. It can also put a lot of pressure on the nervous system making the bird uncoordinated.

Birds can also develop cancers in the lymphatic system. This compromises the immune system to a large extent leading to secondary bacterial, viral or fungal infections. When the tumor is malignant, the condition is known as lymphoma. It is characterized by swollen lymph nodes in most cases.

Another type of tumor in the birds are lipomas. These are made mostly of mature fat cells. You will find these tumors just under the skin of the bird near the abdomen and the chest. They interfere with the body movements and will also lead to lethargy and inactivity. These are normally seen in obese birds.

Tumors that are external are easily identified as they appear in the form of lumps. Any abnormal growth on the body should be shown to the vet immediately. A pathologist will examine samples from the affected area and will determine if it is a tumor or not. The next step is to check if it is malignant or benign.

The internal tumors are really hard to detect. You will notice symptoms like:
- Loss of weight
- Increased sleep
- Loss of appetite
- Inability to balance the body
- Lameness

These symptoms could be indicative of any other disease as well. So, you need to have your bird checked by a vet the moment you notice them.

Treatment of tumors or lipomas includes surgical removal of the mass of cells. If the tumor is growing or changing and is located in a part of the body that can affect its daily activities, surgery is avoided.

Prognosis of benign tumors is definitely better than the malignant ones. It could just require removal of the tissue in most cases.

It is the malignant tumors that are harder to treat. This is because they may continue to spread even after removal, unless they are removed at a very early stage.

Tumors of the kidney, the liver and other vital organs are the hardest to deal with as they could lead to death of the bird during surgery due to excessive bleeding.

In the case of blue macaws, it is a lot easier thanks to the size of the birds. The larger the animal, the easier it is to carry out surgical procedures.

In rare cases, radiation and chemotherapy may help control these malignant tumors. They will be used in conjunction with surgical processes.

This is a very recent practice in avian medicine. That is why most avian vets will have less experience with providing radiation to birds. However, when there are very few avenues of treatment, radiation may be used on an experimental basis.

The drugs used in chemotherapy are very harsh. Since birds are easily susceptible to toxicity, there are chances that the bird dies of poisoning in the course of this treatment.

If the tumor is malignant, there is very little chance of survival unless the bird is treated in the initial stages. That is why it is recommended to take your bird for regular check-ups by the veterinarian. That way the tests will be able to detect internal tumors, if any.

Toxicity

Heavy metal poisoning due to metals like zinc and lead is quite common in pet birds. This is because of the several sources of toxicity that we neglect while getting the house bird proofed.

Zinc poisoning:

The discomfort caused depends upon the amount toxins that are present in the body of the bird. There are some signs of toxicity that you need to watch out for:
- Shallow breathing
- Lethargy
- Anorexia
- Weight loss
- Weakness
- Kidney dysfunction
- Blue or purple coloration of the skin
- Feather picking
- Regurgitation
- Paleness in the mucous membrane
- Excessive consumption of water followed by urination to flush the toxins out.
- Inability to balance the body.

The most common sources of infection are the cages, toys and wires around the cage that are galvanized, washers or nuts made from zinc, pennies that were minted after the year 1983.

Lead poisoning:

Lead poisoning is more fatal as the lead that is absorbed will be retained in the soft tissues of the body. This can cause neural damage and can even lead to problems with the kidneys and the GI system.

The symptoms of lead poisoning are the same as zinc poisoning. But the sources of zinc poisoning are a lot more in comparison. The common sources are tooth brushes, lead paint, lead weight used for curtains, crystal, cardboard boxes, dyes used in newspaper, vinyl or plastic material, stainless glass windows, plumbing material, foils of some champagne bottles etc.

To treat this condition, an injection called Calsenate is administered. This acts like an antidote that will remove the zinc or lead that has entered the body. If the bird has ingested any metal object, it can be removed surgically. The bird must be put on a recommended diet to ensure that the kidneys and the liver do not shut down, making it harder for the metals to be eliminated from the body.

Make sure that your bird is in a safe environment in order to prevent any metal poisoning. If you are unsure of how to do this on your own, you have several professionals who can come to your home and take care of the whole bird proofing process for you.

4. Injuries and first aid

Broken blood feather

- When you are clipping the wings of the bird, sometimes, you can get a blood feather which will lead to profuse bleeding.

- The best way to deal with this is to remove the broken feather entirely. If you are not sure about how to do this, take your bird to the vet.

- First, you need to stop the bleeding. This can be done by applying some flour on the area or by running a styptic pencil on the injured area.

Constricted toes

- This is a very common condition in baby birds. This occurs when the humidity in the brooding or nesting box low.

- The toes of the bird will seem scaly and will lead to a lot of irritation.

- If the condition progresses, blood flow to the affected toe will be cut off and the toe can become dry and will eventually fall off.

- Consult your vet to get a skin cream that can soften the skin. When it is soft enough, the scaly skin can be peeled off carefully.

Crop burn

- This is yet another common condition in baby birds. Luckily it can be resolved quite easily.

- If the crop feathers have not developed yet, the bird is more susceptible to the condition.

- A blister or a patch of white skin is seen on the crop. This is caused by the burn in the crop.

- Make sure that the food that you give your baby bird is the right temperature to prevent crop burn.

- Stir your finger in the food to make sure that there are no hot spots in it.

- If you notice a blister, make sure you call your vet immediately. When left unattended, this condition can be fatal to baby birds.

Dehydration

- This is a condition that can affect your blue macaw at any age. You will notice that the skin is red and is very elastic.

- If you pick the skin slightly, it will stay wrinkled when the bird is dehydrated.

- In baby birds, dehydration can be caused by a bacterial infection that makes digestion slow.

- The first thing that you should do is to rehydrate the bird immediately. The vet can give your bird a Ringers' solution injection to help him recover immediately.

- Adding some apple juice or a fruit that your bird enjoys in the water can urge him to consume water.

- You can even give the bird Pedialyte to restore the water level in the body immediately.

- Make sure that clean and fresh water is available to your bird at all times. Birds will not consume water that may have some fecal matter or debris in it.

Broken wings

- Running into walls, getting caught in ropes used to suspend toys or even a fight can lead to broken wings in birds.

- You will see that the wing hangs down from the side of the body and will also notice that he bird is hesitant to move and will resort to a corner on the floor of the cage.

- The first thing to do is to move the cage to an area that is free from any stress.

- If the bird is not hand trained, then pick him up by wrapping a towel around him.

- Hold the feather in place and tape it in place with guaze. Using surgical tape or sticky tape can damage the feathers.

- Then, rush him to the vet immediately.

Split sternum

- A split sternum occurs when the breast bone breaks and punctures the skin on the chest of the bird.

- This is caused when the bird falls on a hard surface or when he is attacked by another bird or a pet.

- Birds that have clipped wings are prone to this accident.

- The skin on the chest must be sutured and therefore, take the bird to the vet immediately.

- This injury should be prevented by ensuring that the cage is not placed on a hard surface or near one.

Cuts and wounds

- If you see a scrape or wound on the body of the bird, it must be cleaned with an antiseptic solution immediately.

- For a mild cut, you can apply some styptic powder to clot the blood and then apply an antiseptic cream or rinse with hydrogen peroxide.

- If the wound is deep, then hold a piece of gauze on it and apply some pressure. This will control the bleeding while the bird is taken to the vet.

Burns

- Landing on a hot stove or grazing against a hot bulb while flying can lead to burns.

- The burnt area should be held under cold running water to ease to pain.

- If it is a mild burn you can apply a burn cream or antiseptic on the area and allow it to heal.

- In case of severe burns, your bird will need immediate veterinary attention.

Sour crop

- This is a condition that occurs only in baby birds that are being hand fed.

- It is important for the crop to be emptied entirely at least once a day.

- If this does not happen, the food in the crop will begin to spoil and will slow down digestion.

- Inserting a feeding tube to clean the crop is one way to empty it.

- You can also hold the bird upside down and then massage the crop area to push the food out of the mouth. This is risky as it can lead to food getting into the respiratory system if your bird panics.

- If you do not know how to insert the feeding tube, do not attempt to do it as it can rupture the esophagus. Make sure that you consult someone with more experience.

With these common injuries, prevention is definitely better than cure. Make sure that he environment of the bird is safe and that you follow the right techniques of feeding and grooming your bird to prevent accidents.

Preparing a First aid kit

Having a first aid kit is very important to make sure that your bird gets immediate attention when he has an injury or an accident. You must keep a kit with the following items handy at all times:

- Styptic pencil or powder
- Medicated gauze
- Cotton pads
- A small syringe to clean wounds or provide medicines
- Ink dropper

- Tweezers
- A pair of small scissors
- Antiseptic cream recommended by the vet
- Hydrogen peroxide to wash wounds and burns
- Sterile saline solution
- A pair of gloves
- A towel to handle the bird easily
- The number of your vet
- Poison control numbers
- Cotton ear buds to apply ointments and medicines

Alternatively, you can also purchase commercially prepared first aid kids that will be easily available with your vet. Some are also available online. Make sure that you find one that is recommended by your vet to be sure that it contains everything that you will need in case of an emergency.

When your bird is with a pet sitter or is being taken care of by a friend or relative, make sure that you provide them with all the emergency contact details to take care of a sudden medical emergency.

The last and most important thing is to contact your insurance company to find out about options for your blue macaw. There are some insurance companies that your vet will also be able to recommend to cover for any major surgery, unexpected medical needs or even for third party damage caused by your bird.

If you are not able to find a satisfactory insurance policy, you must set aside medical emergency funds for your bird to be prepared for an untoward situation.

5. Insurance for pet birds

Getting pet insurance for birds is not very easy. Most insurance companies will provide policies for cats and dogs, but rarely for birds. However, there are some reliable ones that will give you decent benefits. The most common things that are covered by popular pet insurance are:

- Veterinary charges: They will pay for certain diagnostic procedures like X-rays and even some consultation fees. Veterinarian costs will most include emergencies only. In case of birds like the macaw that have long lives, there may be a limit on the cover offered annually that may go up to $1500 or £3000.

- Escape or Loss/ Death: If you lose your bird to theft or death, they may cover some amount of the market value of an exotic bird. Theft and escape cover requires you to fulfill some security conditions such as purchasing a five lever lock for the cage door.
- Public Liability: This covers any damage caused by your bird to another person or property.
- Overseas covers: This is necessary for you to travel with your pet to some countries.

The cost of your insurance with all these covers will come up to about $150 or £280 a month. These covers are purchased separately and you can cut costs on things like overseas cover or public liability cover if you do not think that it is necessary. However, all these covers are highly recommended for all pet owners. You can compare the costs of various insurance plans online to find one that works for you. If you have multiple birds, some of them may also offer a 10% discount on the insurance cover.

The two most popular insurance plans for macaws are:

- Pet Assure: With this policy you can only have your bird checked by a vet in the network approved by them. If your vet is not part of this network, you need to find one that is or you will not be able to get the cover for vet costs.

- VPI- This insurance does allow you to see any preferred veterinarian. However, they do put a limit on the number of visits and the cover that they offer annually. So, you may not be able to get full coverage for any major procedure that your bird may have to undergo.

That said, there is no policy for birds that is perfect. So, if you want to choose the most reliable one it may be the one that your veterinarian is associated with. That way you can be assured of some cover at least.

Most pet macaw owners will suggest that you alternatively open a savings account for your macaw. This is primarily to be equipped for medical emergencies. In addition to that, some may even tell you not get insurance as it may be too expensive and may not even give you as many benefits. In fact, these insurance premiums can be more expensive that the ones that you have for human beings! However, if you have any travel plans in the future with your macaw, then getting insurance might be mandatory in some countries.

Chapter 7: Cost of Keeping a Blue Macaw

The costs of owning a macaw is a lot more than you can expect. This will depend on the individual species, as some might need specialized and more expensive facilities. The best way forward is to do some research on the bird you are targeting to take in as a pet.

Before committing to a macaw, make sure you have the financial stability to maintain one. With every impulse buy, it is only the bird that suffers. Here is a detailed breakdown of the possible cost associated with macaws.

- Cost of the macaw: $800-10,000 or £400-5000 depending upon the age and the variety of the macaw.

- Cage: $350-600 or £150-400 depending upon the features available and the size. This is a one-time investment and it is recommended that you get the best.

- Food: $40 or £25 every month.

- Toys: This really depends upon the type of toys that you buy. But you will shell out a minimum of $30-50 or £15-25 for sturdy toys for your macaw.

- Wing clipping: About $15 to £10 every four months.

- Veterinarian Cost: You will spend at least $50 or £30 per visit to your veterinarian. You can expect annual costs of about $1200 or £650 per year.

- Pet Insurance: Depending on the kinds of cover that you are getting, your pet insurance may cost anything between $150-280 or £80-150 every month.

Conclusion

Blue Macaws are extremely rare birds and are also expensive. Caring for them requires you to gain information about their specific needs. This book, I hope, provides you with all the assistance that you need with respect to your blue macaw.

The idea behind this book is to ensure that you are a responsible bird owner. That way, your bird will live a happy and healthy life. You will also be able to cherish all the memories that you make with your bird for a lifetime.

It can be tricky to have a bird that is as intelligent as the blue macaw as a pet. But with time, you will be able to figure out what your bird needs and will be able to provide him with all the care he needs.

Thank you for reading this book. If you are a blue macaw owner, then you can be sure that you have a wonderful companion for life.

References

You can never be sure what piece of information comes handy with raising your blue macaw. The Internet has several sources that can help you find the right information. Here are some reliable websites that you can go through as you research about your blue macaw:

- www.macaw-facts.com
- www.bluemacaws.org
- www.animal-world.com
- www.quora.com
- www.cinemablend.com
- www.beautyofbirds.com
- www.bagheera.com
- www.peteducation.com
- www.petparrot.com
- www.parrotsecrets.com
- www.birdtricks.com
- www.au.answers.yahoo.com
- www.neotropical.birds.cornell.edu
- www.rioyou.blogspot.in
- www.avianadventuresaviary.com
- www.hyacinthmacawaviary.com
- www.studentswithbirds.wordpress.com
- www.parrotsinternational.org
- www.pets.thenest.com
- www.sciencedirect.com
- www.informationvine.com
- www.what-when-how.com
- www.animals.nationalgeographic.com
- www.parrotsnaturally.com
- www.parrotscanada.com
- www.adoptapet.com
- www.companionparrots.org
- www.pets.thenest.com
- www.northernparrots.com
- www.windycityparrot.com
- www.pbspettravel.co.uk

www.ingramcontent.com/pod-product-compliance
Lightning Source LLC
Chambersburg PA
CBHW060118050426
42448CB00010B/1928